Publishing Children's Poetry For 19 Years

Bust-A-Rhyme

Giving verse a voice

Bedfordshire & Buckinghamshire

Edited by Allison Jones

First published in Great Britain in 2010 by:

Young Writers
Remus House
Coltsfoot Drive
Peterborough
PE2 9JX
Telephone: 01733 890066
Website: www.youngwriters.co.uk

All Rights Reserved
Book Design by Spencer Hart, Ali Smith & Tim Christian
© Copyright Contributors 2009
SB ISBN 978-184924-821-1

Foreword

Young Writers' Bust-A-Rhyme competition is a showcase for secondary school pupils to share their poetic creativity and inspiration. Selecting the poems has been challenging and immensely rewarding. The effort and imagination invested by these young writers makes their poems a pleasure to enjoy reading time and time again.

Young Writers was established in 1991 to nurture creativity in our children and young adults, to give them an interest in poetry and an outlet to express themselves. Seeing their work in print will encourage them to keep writing and become our poets of tomorrow.

Contents

Cardinal Newman School, Luton
Dearbhla Hubbard (12) 1
Joan Fondong (12) 1
Emily Linda Young (14) 2
Sinéad Duffy (13) 3
Sarah Castleman (13) 4
Eddie Kelly (13) 5
Charlotte Dellow (13) 6
Jasmin Zenobia Woodward (12) 6
Lisah Mataruse (12) 7
Jack Campion (12) 7
Anna Balducci (13) 8
Joseph Green (11) 8
Ellen Aine Scowen (13) 9
Ryan Carabin (11) 9
Leah Widdicombe (13) 10
Jacob Duffy (13) 10
Declan Haylock (14) 11
Oliwia Wojciak (13) 11
Michael Rae (13) 12
Patrick Joy (12) 12
Shaunna McMahon (13) 13
Ella McNabola (12) 13
Calvin Muniafu (12) 14
Liam Treanor (12) 14
Niall Lawn (11) 15
Connor Dunbar (14) 15
Charlotte Kelly (12) 16
James Bruton (11) 16
Harriet Peverall (12) 17
Pheba John (11) 17
Sydney Cornforth (12) 18
Soraya Caraca (11) 18
Niall Gaughan (12) 19
James Lee (14) 19
Dara Robinson (12) 20
Lara Francioni (12) 20
Patrick Ballantyne (12) 21
Ann Marie Orridge (14) 21
Krzysztof Chwesiak (13) 22
Ella Maddox (12) 22
Oliver Burridge (12) 23
Emily Rand (12) 23
Esther Ichanghai (13) 24
Siobhan Ralph (13) 24
Frank Daly (11) 25
Liam O'Shaughnessy (12) 25
Bradley Taylor (12) 26
Ryan Flanagan (12) 26
Jennifer Burke (13) 27
Donna Dowd (13) 27
Anna Rowley (13) 28
Jessica Tyler (13) 28
Anna Gallagher (12) 29
Charlett Daly (12) 29
Jessica Cerasale (12) 29
Michelle Hanson (12) 30
Madison McLoughlin (11) 30
Lynn Nyemba (14) 30
Gabrielle Outram (12) 31
Lewis Potter (11) 31
Joe Keegan (13) 31
Zuzanna Plociennik (12) 32
Lucy Edwardes (11) 32
Carlos Gaddi (11) 32
Laura Perry (13) & Nicola Sheehan 33
Rebecca Copley (11) 33

Chalfonts Community College, Chalfont St Peter
Sophie Bradley (11) 33
Rhiannon Taylor (11) 34
Alfie Franey (11) 34
James Tompkins (11) 35
Erika Anastasia Wedlake (12) 35
Alex Bengougam (11) 36
Megan Clark (11) 36
Georgina Hurman (11) 37
Elena Queally (11) 37
Avril Tricker (11) 38
David Shoesmith (11) 38
Sam Sheard 39

Sabrina Amato (11) ... 39
Ben Wiley (11) ... 40
Millie Grierson (12) ... 40
Sophie May North (11) ... 41
Lucy Campling (11) ... 41
Louis Beever (11) ... 42
Charley Anne Agnes Kendall (12) ... 42
Gemma May Davis (11) ... 43
Emma Shields (11) ... 43
Chelsea Dunstan (11) ... 44
Tom Barlow (11) ... 44
Athena-Skye Finney (11) ... 45
Ciaran Bohan (11) ... 45
Yasmin Rahman (11) ... 46
Reece Tattersall (11) ... 46
J C (11) ... 47
Agata Zakrzewska (11) ... 47
Trudie Mills (11) ... 48
Sarah Davies (11) ... 48
Nathan White (11) ... 49
Jennifer Cox (11) ... 49
Mitko Zyumbyulev (11) ... 50
Ross Alexander Palmer (12) ... 50
Shawnean Milton (11) ... 51
Sharnee Budwal (11) ... 51
Ismail Shariff (11) ... 52
Jacob Barnes (11) ... 52
Shannon Preston (11) ... 52
Thomas Morrissey (11) ... 53
Harry Laflin (11) ... 53
Sinead Hughes (11) ... 53
John Dennis Carey (11) ... 54
Lydia Willison-Duff (11) ... 54
Matthew Bainbridge (12) ... 54
Jonathan Jones (11) ... 55
Isabel Heinel (11) ... 55
Sam Mackerness (11) ... 55
George Boyles (11) ... 56
Kayleigh Gingell (11) ... 56
Cassidy Willson (11) ... 56
Emily Picton (11) ... 57
Rhianna Quirk (11) ... 57
Luke Davison (11) ... 57
Kimran Kaur Kaley (11) ... 58
David Cottrell (11) ... 58
Chrystal Faux (11) ... 58

Highcrest Community School, High Wycombe
Dannii Laine (12) ... 59
Kier Robinson (11) ... 59
Charlotte Louise Helene Lawrence (12) ... 60
Caity Hicks (11) ... 60
Saarah Mohammed (11) ... 61
Xyla Jae Jacobs (11) ... 61
Jeremiah Patel (11) ... 62
Henna Aslam (11) ... 62
Liam Gates (11) ... 63
Emily Burton (11) ... 63
Charles Basham (12) ... 64
Joshua Smith (11) ... 64
Hannah Rendell (11) ... 65
Richard Crawley (12) ... 65
Emma Prince (11) ... 66

Lincroft Middle School, Oakley
Georgia Holloway (11) ... 66
James Gillum (12) ... 67
Abigail Mae Saunders (13) ... 68
James Guinn (13) ... 69
Katy Watson (12) ... 70
Elizabeth Frost (11) ... 71
Katie Webb (11) ... 71
Hannah Burnage (12) ... 72
Anya Williams (12) ... 73
Tom Horn (11) ... 73
Elise Warburton (11) ... 74
David Evans (12) ... 74
Charlie Brittain (12) ... 75
Amy Matthews (11) ... 75
Katy Hobbs (13) ... 76
Chloe Preston (12) ... 77
Edward Williams (12) ... 78
Harriet Pentland (12) ... 79
Matthew Perren (12) ... 79

St Bernard's Catholic School, High Wycombe
Holly O'Brien (11) ... 80
Rebecca Herath (11) ... 80
Glenston D'Silva (12) ... 81

Harmony Sharpe (11)	81
Elizabeth Jones (12)	82
Callum Morris (11)	82
Luis Miguel Oliveira Rocha (11)	83
Charlie Harris (11)	83
Komal Iqbal (11)	84
Freddie Redman (11)	84
Louise Amos (11)	85
John Mark Brenda (11)	85
Kudzai Gayle Chinjekure (11)	86
Laura Pennell (12)	86
Lauren Perry (11)	87
Laxsan Karunanithy (12)	87
Lily Wiggins (12)	88
Alex Gazard (11)	88
Helena Dagnall (11)	89
Daniel Bradley (11)	89
Natalie Samasuwo (13)	90
Adel Brooks (11)	90
Natalie Fawcett (12)	91
Robson Grant (11)	91
Angel Kula (11)	92
Chloe Messenger (11)	92
Amy Barnes (11)	93
Jakub Kopciuch	93
Elliot Leaman (11)	94
Chloe O'Toole (11)	94
Giordano Iaciofano (11)	95
Joan Laight (12)	95

Sharnbrook Upper School, Sharnbrook

Gabby Marinaro (13)	96
Lorna Webb (15)	97
Sophie Hepburn (13)	98
Katie Holyoak (13)	99
Xander De Wit (14)	100
Stuart Reynolds (14)	100
Hannah Bodily (13)	101
Eden Smith (13)	101
Sarah Nash (15)	102
Jamie Bisset (13)	103
Jamie Gibson (15)	104
Sophie Curran (14)	104
Ann Freeman (13)	105

Thomas Tugulu (13)	105
Alice Crawford (18)	106
Rob Arrenberg (15)	106
Dominic Clarke (13)	107
Elliot Jackson-Smith (13)	107
Terrell Conlon (13)	108
Amy Honeywell (15)	108
Jessica Rowley (15) & Clarissa Marston (14)	109
Ricky D Patel (13)	109
Becky Bailey (14)	110
Alice Evans (13)	110
Oliver Seabrook (13)	111
Tom Freed (13)	111
Amy Bishop (15)	112
Jazzy Grove (13)	112
Becky Heath (14)	113
William Slater (13)	113
Kirsty Ireson (13)	114
James Holyoake (13)	114

The Misbourne School, Great Missenden

Abbie Martin (12)	115
Megan Docchar (12)	116
Eleanor Coy (12)	116
Katie Morgans (12)	117
Isabella Handcock (13)	118
J L Rutland (13)	119
Rebecca Towersey (12)	119

The Wye Valley School, Bourne End

Martha Southby (11)	120
Bethany Sparkes (11)	120
Ceire Warren (11)	121
Isha Turner (11)	121
Georgia Scannell (11)	122
Heather Anderson (11)	122
Alistair Beard (12)	123
Amber Healey (12)	123
William Wright (11)	124
Sameeyah Bint-Mahmood (11)	124
Lottie Kirby (11)	124
Migle Kuzaite (12)	125

Megan Hughes (11)	125
Daniel Cleeve (12)	125
Charlotte Anderson (11)	126
Claire Marshall (11)	126

Woodland Middle School, Flitwick

Trudie Reardon (12)	126
Bobby Currie (12)	127
Chloe Potts (12)	128
Reef Brady (11)	128
Melissa Hunt (12)	129
Drew Gillespie (11)	129
Keeleigh Anne Saunders (12)	130
Matthew Wright (12)	130
Sarah Gamble (11)	131
Chris Peters (13)	131
Sherie Titmus (12)	132
Ben Short (11)	132
Isabel Lawton (13)	133
Zoe Sparham (12)	134
Lee Shaw (13)	135
Rhea Biswell (11)	135
Nathan Day (12)	136
Adam Franklin (12)	136
Liza Blackman (12)	137
Connor Wemyss (11)	137
Amy Foley (13)	138
Tommy Smith (11)	138
Alex Sanderson (11)	139
Georgia Pain (11)	139
Kathryn Brandon (13)	140
Shannon Ward (12)	140
Abi Donohue (13)	141
Charlie Cooper (11)	141
Paige Caroline Deacon (12)	142
Mali Ratcliffe (11)	142
Ellie Yip (11)	143
Callum Avern-Love (11)	143
Kelly Morgan (12)	144
Jarrad Miah (11)	144
Chloe Goddard (11)	145
Emily Josephine Wilson (12)	145
Caroline Bates (12)	146
Kelly Newlands (12)	146
Olivia Parrott (11)	147
Coral Harvey (12)	147
Adam Tibbett (11)	148
Louis Brown (11)	148
Niall Vanner (12)	149
Emily Donohue (11)	149
James Williams-Crowther (11)	150
Jonathan Blazeby (11)	150
Josh Ramsay (12)	151
Holly Kirkpatrick (12)	151
Tilly Currer (11)	152
Bethany Thompsett (12)	152
Lauren Wiles (11)	153
Saskia Underwood (12)	153
Aimée Bishop (11)	154
Katie Daw (12)	154
Laura Burgess (12)	155
Daniel Keegan (12)	155
Amber Walker (12)	156
Ryan Pickard (11)	156
Kayleigh Lyon (11)	157
Lauren Ash (11)	157
Jamie Dann (11)	158
Stephanie Fox (12)	158
Heléna Batchelor (11)	159
Thomas Andrew Lark (11)	159
Holly Plenty (12)	160
Aimee Hutchinson (11)	160
Charlotte Lucy Wermerling (12)	161
Thomas Woodcraft (11)	161
Anna Bright (12)	162
Isaac Malkani (11)	162
Zoe Burton (11)	162
Megan Darvall (12)	163
Mitchell Flewers (12)	163
Lucy Elizabeth Rollinson (11)	163
Charlotte Wood (11)	164
Tyler Callum Webb (11)	164

The Poems

He Lies

He lies on the floor, so helpless and poor.
All he wants is a bit more.
All he has is a sheet to sleep.
He hasn't got a bite to eat.
He begs for hours then he just picks flowers.
He can be kind when he uses his mind.

Dearbhla Hubbard (12)
Cardinal Newman School, Luton

Do You Know How It Feels?

Do you know how it feels
To be on the streets
Sitting on seats
Out in the cold
With no one to hold?

Do you know how it feels
To be famished?
It's like being punished,
No money
To buy even honey.
I don't know what to think
But do they have a drink?

But the truth is
You don't know how it feels.

Joan Fondong (12)
Cardinal Newman School, Luton

I'm Sorry

I'm sorry I hurt you,
I'm sorry I tore us apart,
I'm sorry I made you cry,
I'm sorry I broke your heart.

I'm sorry I made you leave me,
I'm sorry I ever said a word,
I'm sorry I split our love in two,
I was out of order, I was absurd.

Please just forgive me,
Our love was so strong,
I'm so lost without you,
I know what I did was wrong.

I'm sorry I never told you,
Treated you like a fool,
The truth is I never knew,
That love could be so cruel.

That other girl was nothing,
No more than a fling,
It's you that I'm in love with,
Flowers, choccies, what else can I bring?

Some say that teenage love
Will never ever last.
I want to show them wrong babe,
I send my apology from the heart.

I've done everything I can to make this mess the past,
I've tried to secure a future, let's give us two another blast.

Emily Linda Young (14)
Cardinal Newman School, Luton

Waiting

I walk down the dark street
Looking around for him
But he is nowhere to be found
My only company, the moon

She told me about her pal, Night
He is very shy and mysterious
Night adores Day
Her sunshine and rainbow of colours

He always tries to catch her
Running as fast as he can
But Dawn and Dusk separate them
The terrible two
They steal the darkness from Night
And the lightness from Day

Patiently we wait
I sit, imagining his arrival
Night anticipates his meeting with Day
We watch the wonderful world around us
Seeing each season melt away

Changes happening everywhere
Yet we stay the same
Still waiting for the day
Thinking what it will be like

When the time will come, unknown
How long we will wait, a mystery
What we will do in-between . . .

Sinéad Duffy (13)
Cardinal Newman School, Luton

The Sound On The Streets

I was walking down the street
When I heard a sudden sound
It sounded really strange and it made me turn around
I looked about the street but nothing that I saw
Was anywhere as frightening,
As that sound I'd heard before,
Then I heard it again, by the corner of the shops,
It sounded really scary, like a frog with a cough,
This time I got frightened, and started to run
But he jumped out in front, so at him I shunned,
Slowly but carefully I tried to edge round,
Then he made a noise and I knew he was the sound,
So I started to run towards my home, as fast as I could,
So he couldn't catch me, and escape I would,
Eventually I just had to slow,
Then I knew he was coming, fast as he could go,
I could somehow feel it, deep in my bones,
So again I was running,
Towards my home,
I got inside and locked the door
Then I heard the sound that I'd heard before,
I screamed and cried then ran to my room
But only to find
I'd run to my doom!
So be safe on the streets
Cos you never know
Just what could happen
When you're on your way home.

Sarah Castleman (13)
Cardinal Newman School, Luton

The Lonely Girl

She's depressed and lonely,
Skinny and bony.
Suicidal but scared,
Because no one cared.

I will help her,
I will comfort her.
I will hold her,
Because I love her.

She's not alone,
She now has a home.
With me forever,
Separated never.

I will help her,
I will comfort her.
I will hold her,
Because I love her.

And when our end is near,
Let's spend it together.
Because our love will go on,
Forever and ever.

I will help her,
I will comfort her.
I will hold her,
Because I love her.

Eddie Kelly (13)
Cardinal Newman School, Luton

Broken

Fear of the dark,
Tears her world apart.
The dreams in her head,
A perfect illusion from the heart.

Pressure takes over,
Grasping her by the throat.
Her head is like a bomb,
Waiting to explode.

Eyes pass straight through her,
She's unnoticed by the world.
With destruction on her shoulders,
Her cries no longer heard.

The mind has been poisoned,
By meaningless games.
Burning a hole deep inside her,
The strengthening flames.

Forever falling,
Crawling to retreat.
Everybody's victory,
Results in her defeat.

Mystery surrounds the soul like a magical mist,
Alas, a broken spirit can very rarely be fixed.

Charlotte Dellow (13)
Cardinal Newman School, Luton

Life

Can you see the painful tears lurking in my eyes?
Every time you look at me I see the dreadful lies.
My life is smashed like shards of glass,
And when I lay them down on the grass
I look at the depressing life I've lived
And all the things I've had to give
To receive nothing in return . . .
Next time maybe I will learn.

Jasmin Zenobia Woodward (12)
Cardinal Newman School, Luton

People

People are black
People are white
People are yellow
People are green
> But hey no one's looking

People are rich
People are poor
People are average
People are millionaires
> But hey no one's looking

People are clever
People are vain
People are slow
People are intelligent
> But hey no one's looking

People are Christian
People are Muslim
People are Jews
People are Satanic
> But hey no one's looking

Because we are all connected as one
There is still hope on Earth.

Lisah Mataruse (12)
Cardinal Newman School, Luton

The Bullet

A bullet flies through the air
The bullet gives the nation a scare
The bullet destroys all in its way
I wonder who the bullet will kill today.

The bullet is strong and fast
All it takes is one blast
The bullet flies past its prey
The bullet has murdered again today.

Jack Campion (12)
Cardinal Newman School, Luton

Little Brothers

They're here
Then they're there
But then you see them everywhere
You say they won't go away
But people just say oh my gosh no way
They don't believe you
And you say to yourself
Who'd have thought that little bros could get you so distraught
They are really annoying
And can be soooo boring
They like to hide and move your stuff
Then you get into a huff
You get the blame for the things they've done
Then you shout, 'You better run!'
You chase them around and around
Then we hear an ear-piercing sound
Oh no! We better start to run
Because coming up the stairs is our very angry mum
But at the end of the day
You can truly say
They're annoying and boring
They move your stuff
But really they are good enough to love.

Anna Balducci (13)
Cardinal Newman School, Luton

Poverty

Poor little infant
No roof over his head
No parents
No family
No money
No education
No life
Relying on people to satisfy his need
Relying on people to clothe him and to feed.

Joseph Green (11)
Cardinal Newman School, Luton

Abuse To Mankind!

Why is it when something goes right
Something else goes wrong?
Why is life like a tornado waiting to happen?
Why is it arguing and fighting upsets me so much?
Why do people have to be so cruel?

My life is like an egg waiting to crack,
Bruises and cuts, even a smack.
The hurt crawling through my mind can make me cry
But most of the time it just makes me sigh.

I go to my bedroom and I slam my door.
I can feel my bruises, they're so very sore.
My parents don't even care.
All they can do is give me that glare.

They hit me, they hurt me.
They don't see what they are doing to me.
My bruises and cuts show in the light
But no one seems to see the sight.

People are cruel, people are mean,
But sometimes they can be seen.
Not mine, just a crime.
Apparently, the tornado has just begun . . .

Ellen Aine Scowen (13)
Cardinal Newman School, Luton

Homeless Living

Homeless people living on the streets
With their freezing cold bare feet
Lots of people dying
Many hungry children crying

Everywhere you turn they lay
There, they stay living a dreadful day
Why they have this gloomy life we don't know
But we are certainly not their foe.

Ryan Carabin (11)
Cardinal Newman School, Luton

Seasons Of Love

While under the cherry blossom trees,
Tears running down my face.
Head in my hands, falling down to my knees,
I want to be with him, not alone in this place.

Hot blazing sun, making me sweat,
Now we're back together again.
He's teasing me like I'm some sort of pet,
But I want to be his Barbie and he my Ken.

Red, orange and yellow are flashing by,
Trying to be silent, but my heart keeps beating.
I can see him and another girl out the corner of my eye.
The pain is unbearable, I can't believe what I'm seeing.

My feet crunching in the soft snow,
I'm fed up with this pain.
I'm going to jump from this building and I want you to know,
That I still love you and you make me go insane.

Love changes just like seasons do
And it also has its reasons too.

Leah Widdicombe (13)
Cardinal Newman School, Luton

Untitled

I'm sorry for being mean
I'm sorry for not being me
I'm sorry for not being there for you
I'm sorry for not being true
I'm sorry for leaving you in a time of need
I'm sorry for being a teen.

I'm sorry for crying over nothing
I'm sorry for not doing something
I'm sorry for everything that has left me and you so mad
I'm sorry so I'll try never to be bad
I'm sorry Mum and Dad for the terrible life I put you through
I'm sorry.

Jacob Duffy (13)
Cardinal Newman School, Luton

No Future

Waking up to a brain-rattling siren from my alarm clock,
Nothing to get up for anymore,
Same people,
Same routine.

I drag myself out of bed,
Just to see the grey and lifeless concrete jungle on my doorstep,
No future for me in England anymore,
Not that I want a future in England anymore.

Shut my eyes on the tube just long enough to remember home,
Remember the time sitting around the log fire during the bitter winter months,
Listening to my parents' stories of their childhood,
The smell of my mother's cooking lingering in the air.

Then I get knocked to the side by another man in a suit in a hurry
And brings me crashing back to reality,
The same boring life,
The life I don't want,
But the life I need.

Declan Haylock (14)
Cardinal Newman School, Luton

World Without Colour

Imagine what it would be like,
If the world was black and white.
Imagine not seeing the colours of summer,
All the leaves that are green or the colourful flowers.
Imagine walking on a path,
Without being able to laugh,
Because everything would be black and white,
Because everything would be boring.
Nothing would be the same,
The rainbow would lose its colours
Like a bird in the rainforest.
World without colour is not making sense.
Sense is the colour and the colour is life.

Oliwia Wojciak (13)
Cardinal Newman School, Luton

I Don't Care!

I don't care if you think I'm a nobody or that I'm lame.

D o you really think that you can degrade me or humiliate me?
O bviously you think that I'm an easy target because you're not trying to torment anyone else.
N ever will I bow to you or show respect for what you do!
T ell me I'm a loser, tell me what you think, keep it coming I've got time to wait.
C arry on! You're only boring me to death, you're not bullying me, you're just wasting your breath.
A ctually you're the one who's damn well lame! You're just jealous because I'm smarter than you. You're pathetic!
R eally? Is that all you've got? Calling me one single name? I can do better than that! But I won't because I'm the better man and I'm not fighting back!
E very day you try to make me feel blue, by making fun of my family, my friends or just the person who I am, but to be honest you can talk to the hand!

You get the message?

Michael Rae (13)
Cardinal Newman School, Luton

On The Street

Homeless, homeless
Living on the street
Homeless, homeless
With nothing on my feet

Crimes, crimes
Injured here and there
Crimes, crimes
No one with a care

Slavery, slavery
Locked away
Slavery, slavery
But what can I say!

Patrick Joy (12)
Cardinal Newman School, Luton

What Is School For?

What is school for?
Is it to learn new things?
Is it to make friends?
Is it to have fun
Or is it to have the education we need?

What is school for? What is school for?
Please can someone tell me?

What is school for?
Is it to behave with respect?
Is it to listen carefully?
Is it to understand the world around us
Or is it to become the best we can be?

What is school for?
I shall tell you what I think.

School is for helping us to become the best we can be.
School is for anything, as long as we want to learn.

Shaunna McMahon (13)
Cardinal Newman School, Luton

Thunder And Lightning

Like chains clanging
Crash! Boom! Bang!
The terrible sound
Thunders down
The loudest sound you could ever hear
It scares little children
Whenever it's here

They start to cry
And their mother asks them why
But it's because of the sound
That is not stopping
They do not like it
And are terrified of it
Will it ever stop?

Ella McNabola (12)
Cardinal Newman School, Luton

Earth

Our Earth is big,
Like the universe.
But we have a problem,
The Earth has a curse.

People that care,
Want to make a change.
But there are others,
Who aren't even bothered.

Animals, innocent animals,
Are being killed.
Our ozone layer,
Needs to be sealed.

We need to think about
What we should do.
Or the world will go,
Just like you.

Calvin Muniafu (12)
Cardinal Newman School, Luton

Goal!

He passed down the wing
Crosses it in
He headers it down
Bouncing off the ground
The goalkeeper dives in the air
Missing the ball by a hair
It goes in
It's a goal
The crowd roars
With glee and joy

It's 1-0
The whistle goes
The match is over

Finally, I can go.

Liam Treanor (12)
Cardinal Newman School, Luton

War

Bombings are happening everywhere,
Black smoke spreads in the air,
Schools, homes and people suffer,
In the end they will not recover.

Children don't laugh but cry,
As the planes soar across the sky,
It's hard to know when it will end,
As more and more soldiers descend.

Innocent people are dying,
As we all keep trying,
When I look around,
Death is the terrible sound.

I don't think it will be the same,
Unless they end this stupid game,
My hope will never die,
Until they call a successful cry.

Niall Lawn (11)
Cardinal Newman School, Luton

Poverty

Children crying, people dying,
The tears to my eyes.

Sniffing around the bins,
Like wolves ready to kill,
A piece of meat, rushing to get their bit.

Africa, Ethiopia, even England,
Dirty clothes, peaceful minds, not wanting any harm,
Disaster, dreadful, destruction,
All the words in my head.

Sun warmer, hearts colder,
Do they have the will to carry on?
Pray for them, help them, give to them,
Lend them your pockets.

Connor Dunbar (14)
Cardinal Newman School, Luton

Poverty

A child shivers on a street corner,
On a long and lonely night.
Her family dead, she has nothing,
Her eyes are wide with fright.

Not very far away,
An earthquake has struck.
Widespread devastation,
Many have bad luck.

On the next continent,
A war has begun.
Soldiers attack the village,
People flee their homes and run.

Poverty has killed many people,
Spreading worldwide.
So please give a contribution,
It's up to you to decide.

Charlotte Kelly (12)
Cardinal Newman School, Luton

The Lonely Wanderer

Children with nothing to eat
Not one treat.

All those children out there
No one to care.

Not a mum, not a dad
No one to make them glad.

Nowhere to stay
Not one day.

This is the way to act
And this is a fact.

So let's give care
And be fair.

James Bruton (11)
Cardinal Newman School, Luton

Guides!

Guides - what fun!
I have a good laugh.
I meet my friends
And we make up a dance.

Guides - so great!
I go every Friday.
I love to do things
That make me smile.

Guides - how exciting!
Something to look forward to.
I love playing around
And doing what I want to do.

Guides - what fun!
Guides - so great!
Guides - how exciting!
Guides - makes my day!

Harriet Peverall (12)
Cardinal Newman School, Luton

Being Poor

I'm a poor girl from India,
I have a very hard life.
My parents are sending me to work
I think it's very unfair.
I live in a small hut with only one room
And a hearth for all the cooking I do.
In an early morning I go outside and do all the chores
Which takes a very long time.
Then I go to the market, there is hardly any food.
I have a meal and nothing else.
I go picking tea in the roasting sun
And then the evening's for weaving baskets.
The water is dirty, I'm getting terminal diseases,
It's a very hard life being poor like me.

Pheba John (11)
Cardinal Newman School, Luton

Splash!

I jump,
Falling down, down, down deep,
But I am not scared.
I reach the bottom and wait,
I watch my hair float around,
Without gravity.
Watching bubbles race each other to the top,
But still I wait.
I wait until,
I can wait no more,
My lungs on fire,
My eyes burning.
I start to rise,
Looking at my own little world,
But someone, always someone spoils it.
They kick past shattering my lovely world.
My world no more!

Sydney Cornforth (12)
Cardinal Newman School, Luton

Knife In Hand

They get too bullied that they just can't take it,
They get out a knife and may even make it,
They walk out into the night,
Ready to give their enemy a fright,
They walk through the streets,
Scaring everyone they meet,
They knock on the door,
Pushing their enemy to the floor,
They slash and they stab,
Going crazy like mad,
They go on their way,
As the night turns to day,
They look at the sun,
Knowing that their work is now done.

Soraya Caraca (11)
Cardinal Newman School, Luton

Same Old Poverty Ruining Lives

Loads of people are homeless because of war,
They can't buy a home as they are poor.
Some travel around from place to place,
Where really they are in a really big maze.

They face natural disasters every day,
Tsunamis, earthquakes and even hurricanes.
This can tear families apart,
Then they have to make a new start.

Some people will not eat today,
As we just munch and munch away.
They will have to walk miles for safe water to drink.

There are loads of charities helping their fate,
So why don't you just donate?
Cafod, Noah and Children in Need,
Please help them now, you've heard them plead.

Niall Gaughan (12)
Cardinal Newman School, Luton

The Sinking Hands

I do not grab the sinking hands,
When I'm the one who floats,
I do not clothe the naked hands,
When I have many coats.
I do not feed the hungry hands,
When I have food to spare,
I do not help the crying hands,
Instead I choose to stare.
I do not wash the dirty hands,
When I can clean my own,
I do not care for the newborn hands,
When mine have already grown.
I do not give to the needy hands,
For on them I look down,
But when my hands are those that sink,
I am left to drown.

James Lee (14)
Cardinal Newman School, Luton

A Better Place

I lay there . . . waiting, waiting
The sun had been swallowed by the clouds and the dark,
Slowly, slowly . . .
Creeping over the land flinging stars into the sky my mind was in
Other places, happy places of dreams and imagination . . .
While my body lay still, still, stiff, stopped
And my eyes were shut, like blinds covering a window or a blanket,
Wrapping that soft bundle of joy, guarding them from the cold,
Cold, cold . . .
And as I lay there dreaming of the sun's rays on my face
And the soft snowflake on my nose and the pot of gold on
The other side of the rainbow,
My body slowly froze,
And I was taken by the winged saints of the holy place,
To a better world,
A better place . . .

Dara Robinson (12)
Cardinal Newman School, Luton

Christmas Is Here!

Snow falling from the clouds,
As white as cotton wool,
As cold as ice,
Wellie boots, scarves and gloves,
Christmas is near!
Christmas holidays finally here,
Wrapping and receiving,
Decorations and cards,
Christmas is near!
Christmas Eve, Boxing Day,
Excitement, joy and laughter,
Roast dinner and chocolate,
As much as you want,
Christmas was near,
Christmas was here,
Christmas is over until next year!

Lara Francioni (12)
Cardinal Newman School, Luton

Bedfordshire & Buckinghamshire

The Birds In The Sky

The birds in the sky
How high they can fly,
Oh it makes me cry
The birds in the sky
Mr Magpie,
As high as you can fly.
The bird is small, sky high,
Firefly,
As fast as light,
As dark as night,
As quick as flight,
Bird flight.
The bird oh it wanders
As sly as anacondas,
Oh how it flies
Birdflight.

Patrick Ballantyne (12)
Cardinal Newman School, Luton

Where Am I? Where Am I? You May Ask

A place of wonders and awe,
Somewhere I can show my inner self.
A place where everyone lives in harmony,
Somewhere it's OK to be different,
Where am I? Where am I? You may ask.

A place where no tears will fall from your eyes,
Somewhere no one will ever hurt or harm you,
A place where all your dreams come true,
Somewhere full of lust and love,
Where am I? Where am I? You may ask.

A place that seems like a wish upon a star,
Somewhere you can be yourself,
A place that you can enjoy no matter what you look like,
Somewhere 'normal' is not a word,
Where am I? Where am I? You may ask.

Ann Marie Orridge (14)
Cardinal Newman School, Luton

My Dog Sleeping

My dog is sleeping in its bed,
As always it does after it's fed.
It's probably showing its shiny fur,
Trying to show off as if someone will care.
Its small brown nose moving from time to time,
Looking as if someone's committing a crime.
Like waking it up from a great dream,
Stories like no creature had ever seen.

But it's just sleeping, calm as the sea,
Being in its favourite place to be.
In its bed, its home, its house,
Staying as quiet and calm as a mouse.
And soon it stops the dream
And the stories are forgotten and never going to be seen,
Again . . .

Krzysztof Chwesiak (13)
Cardinal Newman School, Luton

He Said, She Said!

A girl asked a boy, 'Would you ever go out with me?'
A boy said, 'No!'
A girl asked a boy, 'Would you ever love me?'
A boy said, 'No.'
A girl asked a boy, 'If I died would you be sad?'
A boy said, 'No.'
A girl asked a boy, 'If I went away, would you wait for me?'
A boy said, 'No.'
The girl said, 'Why not?'
The boy said, 'I wouldn't ever go out with you, I will always go out with you, I wouldn't ever love you, I will always love you, if you died I wouldn't be sad, I would be devastated, if you went away I wouldn't wait for you, I would run after you.
This is because I love you.'

Ella Maddox (12)
Cardinal Newman School, Luton

Army

Dropping out of the aeroplane
Out into the rain,
Onto the ground guns blazin'
My army are erasin'
Any threat of the enemy.

Bullets flying all around
Killing people on the ground
My teammates are surrendering
But I'm not giving up for anything.

This fight will not be over
Until I become your supernova
A nuclear bomb to end this war
But I'm afraid it will kill us all.

Oliver Burridge (12)
Cardinal Newman School, Luton

Autumn - Haikus

The leaves fall from trees,
From branches onto the floor,
It looks very bare!

Yellow, orange leaves,
Sunrise, dawn, sunset, night-time,
Shiver, it is cold!

Winter creeping near,
Getting your jumpers and coats,
Wellie boots and more!

Grass as green as limes,
Sun like a golden balloon,
Sky like tomatoes.

Emily Rand (12)
Cardinal Newman School, Luton

Friends

I have many friends,
Most of them aren't for me;
I'm a real person pleaser; but I'm no pushover
Anyone can see.

Some of my friends are sycophants.
Some of my friends are noisy, loud and rude.
Some of my friends could be elephants; although I can't be too sure.
Some of my friends are weird and crazy, saying that, I am too.

I'm all these things; I take up different traits depending on who I'm with.
I love my friends, they're on what my life depends.
My friendships I hope will never end, life for me is win or lose.

I have many friends, I have lots of fun no matter which I choose.

Esther Ichanghai (13)
Cardinal Newman School, Luton

It's Time To Say Goodbye

They call me names
I don't know what to do
I'm fed up with my life
This has to be true!

I've always been bullied
Since the age of nine
I'm fed up with my life
But everyone says it will be fine.

I can't cope with this anymore
I just want to die
I'm fed up with my life
It's time to say goodbye . . .

Siobhan Ralph (13)
Cardinal Newman School, Luton

Poverty Poem

Poverty shouldn't be,
Everybody can see.
Raise some money,
Come on honey.
We can do this together,
Make a difference forever.
Let's stop poverty now.

Just think of all the things we can do,
Get everyone in on it too.
We can do something good,
Really I think we could.
Get rid of poverty now!

Frank Daly (11)
Cardinal Newman School, Luton

My Dog Ate My Homework!

'My dog ate my homework,' I told everyone.
'My dog ate my homework and my last bun.'
'My dog ate my homework,' but nobody will believe
That my dog ate my homework and my shirt sleeve!
'My dog ate my homework,' I said as I ate.
'My dog ate my homework, I used it as bait,
To get him to come for a walk yesterday.'
But now I'm in big trouble anyway!
I went to the headmaster, he said, 'Oh my word!
That's the worst excuse I've ever heard!'
'But Sir, it is true! My dog ate my homework,
Then he went to the loo!'

Liam O'Shaughnessy (12)
Cardinal Newman School, Luton

Just A Day

Big, black, never-ending
Little white dots like bird droppings on a window
You always see it move
Slowly, quietly, never fast or loud
It's a robber sneaking
Sly and not easily caught
It starts in the east and travels to the west
Like background being pulled from left to right
In the morning it creeps away taking away its darkness
As it goes away
The sun wakes, jumps out of bed and works for another day
Just a day.

Bradley Taylor (12)
Cardinal Newman School, Luton

I Need You

I need you
Like a train needs a track
I need you
Like a cave needs a bat
I need you
Like a bullet needs a gun
I need you
Like bubble needs gum
I need you
Like Harry Hill needs hair
I need you
Like I need underwear.

Ryan Flanagan (12)
Cardinal Newman School, Luton

Why?

War is everywhere
So much hate, no care.
People finding it fun to kill
The thought makes me feel ill.
Your whole life destroyed
Leaving you confused, upset, annoyed.
It's so stupid, can you remember what it's about?
I wish they could discuss their issues before acting out.
Making the world a better place is not hard if we all try
Just a little thing to keep the world ticking by.
Forgive and forget
Don't live your whole life full of regrets.

Jennifer Burke (13)
Cardinal Newman School, Luton

Why Me?

You've got a sting in your tail,
And you'll get me without fail,
Like a thorn in my side,
I've got nowhere to hide.
There's a name for your kind, you're a bully,
If I'm not to your liking you'll tell me why and make me cry.
Does it make you feel better?
It doesn't me.
You've never been strong just aggressive and weak,
You've never liked me because I'm kind and meek,
They say school years are meant to be fun,
But this just seems like a battle that can never be won!

Donna Dowd (13)
Cardinal Newman School, Luton

Olly, Holly, Pat!

There once was a mouse called Olly,
He had a wife called Holly.
It began to rain,
What a pain!
So they had to put up a brolly.

They had a friend called Pat,
He was a cat,
Quite an unusual pair,
But they didn't seem to care.
They just carried on playing cat and mouse
Around the old man's house.

Anna Rowley (13)
Cardinal Newman School, Luton

Why?

Why must I sit in the shadows,
Nobody to turn to,
Only my own heartbeat as comfort?
Why do I sleep hungry, hurting,
The pain of loss seethes through my bones,
Stains of tears scar my face?
Why won't my body give in?
I can't take anymore,
Why won't this life end?
It's like a never-ending song,
Always haunting me.

Jessica Tyler (13)
Cardinal Newman School, Luton

One Heart

One heart, one mind, one body, one soul,
One passion, flowing with my blood,
His eyes, my intake of breath,
Her hand in his,
My heart, in two,
Such confusion. What to do?

She smiles at me, but her eyes are cold,
Her twisted love, is getting old,
When will he realise, try to discover,
The everlasting love, I try hard to cover?

Anna Gallagher (12)
Cardinal Newman School, Luton

That Little Old Man With A Boat!

There was an old man with a boat,
Who was so happy to be afloat,
But when he looked down,
He thought he would drown,
So he never got back in the boat!

That little old man with the boat,
Who is still scared to go afloat,
Rented a dingy,
Pulled the lever thingy
And finally went afloat!

Charlett Daly (12)
Cardinal Newman School, Luton

The Sun And The Sea

The sun is a golden balloon
Throwing its rays like darts
Down on the matchstick-made figurines of people below
The throbbing heat skims the top of the deep azure water
Glittering as it spirals gracefully up the banks.

Jessica Cerasale (12)
Cardinal Newman School, Luton

Rainbows And Fairy Tales

They say at the end of a rainbow there is a pot of gold;
But I have experience, it's actually a field of mould!
All fairy tales have a happy ending;
But the ones I've read, have really left me trembling . . .
I'm like Rapunzel stuck in her tower waiting for her call.
Cinderella sweeping hour after hour,
Waiting for the story to be told.
Poor Sleeping Beauty sleeping in her chamber
Wondering if she'll ever get old!
So, not *all* fairy tales have a happy ending!

Michelle Hanson (12)
Cardinal Newman School, Luton

Poverty Everywhere

It happens almost everywhere,
Some people have hardly anything to wear.
Some people have nothing to eat,
Or anything to wear on their feet.
If only they had opportunities like us,
Maybe they wouldn't make such a fuss.
They just need somewhere to stay for the night,
Away from the hatred and where people fight.
Someone needs to open a door,
So they can have a better life than before.

Madison McLoughlin (11)
Cardinal Newman School, Luton

Flower Petals

He loves me, he loves me not
He loves me, he loves me not
These petals are at fault
For he must love me
For I love him.

Lynn Nyemba (14)
Cardinal Newman School, Luton

Stop Drinking

I listen to them screaming every night and day
I can't believe what's happening, withering your life away.
I can see all your hatred, lurking in your eyes
You're the one I mostly hate and the one I despise,
I can't control my feelings and you can't control your actions.
I don't know what to do with all my reactions,
I cannot tell you what I really feel about you
Because if I do I won't forgive you for what you will do,
I know I do love you really
But many can't wait for the day you stop drinking.

Gabrielle Outram (12)
Cardinal Newman School, Luton

Christmas Child

Christmas is coming, everybody is running
Apart from the people in Africa
Just give a gift, we have loads to shift
And give it to the people in Africa
Fill it with love up from above
And give it to the people in Africa
Christmas is here everybody cheer
Even the people in Africa!

Lewis Potter (11)
Cardinal Newman School, Luton

Crisis

Lonely and frail,
Our country is turning stale.
We care too much about war and invasion
Whilst the homeless are sleeping at railway stations.
Hungry and desperate, sick and in need,
But we carry on as if there's no one to feed.
Nobody cares about the environment
Even though wildlife is turning silent . . .

Joe Keegan (13)
Cardinal Newman School, Luton

The Sun Is Bright

The sun is bright,
Light as gold,
Shining high,
Above on us all,
It's like a big bright yellow balloon,
Way up in the sky,
Smiling down at you,
Sparkling bright and warm too.

Zuzanna Plociennik (12)
Cardinal Newman School, Luton

Poverty Poem

Many people are dying
Their children are crying
Because they have nowhere to live
All they want is a family with love to give
If they could have a bed to sleep in
If they could have some food
If someone would open the door
They would have a better life than before.

Lucy Edwardes (11)
Cardinal Newman School, Luton

Poverty

Can poverty happen to anyone?
Kids and adults?
Can poverty happen in different ways?
Natural disaster, can it make people homeless?
War, can it lead to people being homeless and dying?
Can poverty be stopped by donating money to charities?
Will the money help decrease poverty?
Will poverty be stopped?

Carlos Gaddi (11)
Cardinal Newman School, Luton

Black And White

Everyone scared of what colour they are
What are people gonna do if they take it too far?
If you're black or white, orange or blue,
Doesn't matter the colour, it's what you do.
Why separate? We're all the same,
All together like a burning flame.
We should all care about each other
Like a mum, dad, sister or brother.

Laura Perry (13) & Nicola Sheehan
Cardinal Newman School, Luton

The Earth Takes Its Course

The trees are speaking to us through the wind.
The leaves are dancing on the ground,
The birds are singing and flying through the clouds.
Let nature take its course,
The wind speaks to us through the air.
Water dances in the sea, waves crash on the rocks,
Let nature take its course.

Rebecca Copley (11)
Cardinal Newman School, Luton

Cats And Dogs

I once knew a dog,
Who had a cat.

He chased the cat,
With his bat.

But it ended the wrong way,
For the cat caught the dog.

I now know a cat,
Who has a dog.

The dog serves the cat,
And that is that!

Sophie Bradley (11)
Chalfonts Community College, Chalfont St Peter

The Environment

Global warming,
That's a warning!

All the Earth is turning red
And most of the polar bears are all dead.

So, if we save more electricity,
We won't feel in such a pity.

Global warming,
That's a warning!

The sea level is getting higher,
Our world has been set on fire!

So if you find yourself frowning,
You are in the sea drowning!

Global warming,
That's a warning!

So, if you're cold, wear a cardigan,
Instead of putting the heating on!

Rhiannon Taylor (11)
Chalfonts Community College, Chalfont St Peter

Winter, Summer, Autumn, Spring

Winter, perfect time for fires
But some people prefer to freeze playing in the snow
Making loads of snowmen.

Summer, perfect time for going to the beach
And eating loads of ice cream
But sometimes the sun's so hot you can't bear it.

Autumn, cold and not very colourful
All the leaves falling, leaving the trees bare
And all the flowers dying.

Spring, most amazing time of the year
All the flowers growing, all of them healthy and nice
Perfect time for walking.

Alfie Franey (11)
Chalfonts Community College, Chalfont St Peter

Seasons

Winter is quite annoying, it's cold
And you have to wear so many clothes
We all look forward to Christmas
And hope that it snows

Making lots of snowmen
Falling snow around and around
Heaving the second and third ball on top of the first
Then it all falls into a mound

Spring is so beautiful
With all the flowers growing
Lots and lots of bright, bright colours
When the grass gets long, start mowing

Summer's when it's really hot
With lots of fun and games
You can have a massive water fight
With all the sun, a ball of flames.

James Tompkins (11)
Chalfonts Community College, Chalfont St Peter

Friends And Family

They make you laugh, they make you smile
They give you gifts once in a while
You share secrets, you share your friends
Family are special and so are friends.

Friends
Friends are people that you can chat with, laugh with and share with
Friends are people you can confide with
Friends can have good days, friends can have bad ones
But one thing I know, is that a good, true friend will keep coming back.

Family
I am very lucky people would say
As I have a family who love me in many special ways
We have our ups and we have downs
But we always know that we will always be around.

Erika Anastasia Wedlake (12)
Chalfonts Community College, Chalfont St Peter

A Life Full Of . . .

A life full of war,
What a horrible life it would be!
Guns, knives, bombs,
What a horrible life it would be!

A life full of happiness,
What a wonderful life it would be!
Smiling, laughter, love,
What a wonderful life it would be!

A life full of pain,
What a horrible life it would be!
Disease, heartbreak, death,
What a horrible life it would be!

A life full of peace,
What a wonderful life it would be!
Handshakes, plants, animals,
What a wonderful life it would be!

Alex Bengougam (11)
Chalfonts Community College, Chalfont St Peter

The Sting Of Death

She lies there
Swimming in a pool of blood
Her skin pale as a cloud
Her body sunken to the ground
The scream haunts the surrounding
Spirits rise
She lies there . . . dead

He lies there
Choking on his own blood
Begging for mercy
The bullet sits proud in pain
His shiver runs along the ground
Fingertips rest
He lies there . . . dead.

Megan Clark (11)
Chalfonts Community College, Chalfont St Peter

Seasonal Greetings

Autumn has come around again
Wondering when the raining leaves will end
Slipping on last year's wellies
I want to stay in and watch the telly

After autumn comes the winter snow
Dad is tutting at the grass that he can't mow
I, however, am in a snowball war
Oops! I threw one at nextdoor's door!

Look outside, spring has come around
Blossom from the tree hits the ground
Newborn lambs, cows and chicks
They're really cute, I want to take a pic

Summer is here, listen to the cheer
Ready to go in first gear
Splashing around, swimming in a pool
This is the best season after all!

Georgina Hurman (11)
Chalfonts Community College, Chalfont St Peter

Snow

Snow, snow, it comes in as a patrol,
It takes you down,
Like one frostbite!
It never seems to calm you,
It makes you out of control,
Like one, two, three . . . and
Snowballs everywhere,
 and in your hair,
It's the snow we love,
It comes out as white as a dove.

And when it comes to Christmastime,
We all sing a happy rhyme,
It's Christmas that we love,
Christmas in the snow.

Elena Queally (11)
Chalfonts Community College, Chalfont St Peter

Sweets

Gummy drops and lollipops
I love sweets.
Candyfloss and ice cream slosh
Give me more please.
Chocolate bars and Milky Stars
I love sweets.
Cupcakes and sugar bakes
I just can't resist.
Chocolate chips and chewing strips
I love sweets.
Sticky toffee, Costa coffee
Give me more please.
Strawberry tarts and Haribo stars
I love sweets.
Doughnut rings and sugar things
I love sweets!

Avril Tricker (11)
Chalfonts Community College, Chalfont St Peter

The Goal!

Run, run, run
With the ball
'Pass, pass, pass!'
The striker screams
But no, you go it alone
The old stepover
Round the defender
One more defender left
Go, go, go
Burst of speed
Past the defender
Goalkeeper to beat
I pull back my foot
It's like a rocket
Goal, goal, goal
The crowd goes wild, I scored!

David Shoesmith (11)
Chalfonts Community College, Chalfont St Peter

Music

I like listening to music that is really bad
It makes me cry and really sad
I like to listen to music that is happy
But I assure you, it won't make me sappy.
I like listening to heavy metal
It makes me crazy and mental
I like listening to rap
Because it makes me want to clap, clap, clap.
I like listening to classical
Some people think it's slow, but I think it's radical
I like listening to R 'n' B
Rhianna, Snoop Dog and Big D.
I like listening to music, it makes me smile
I will listen to it for a long while
Classic, R 'n' B, heavy metal, bad
It all makes me happy, crazy and sad!

Sam Sheard
Chalfonts Community College, Chalfont St Peter

Glorious Seasons

Winter is a graceful season
The leaves are covered in snow
And the children are covered in clothes.

Summer is a nice time, but spring comes first
Spring is quite a time, the flowers start to bloom
And the leaves start to grow.

Summer is a hot time
The flowers are nicely bloomed
And are sunbathing in the scorching hot sun.

Autumn ends everything
The leaves change colour
And eventually fall out.

The seasons are quite nice
But they end so you have to wait till next year.

Sabrina Amato (11)
Chalfonts Community College, Chalfont St Peter

Football

Full of so much fun,
Football is a game,
Football is a competition
And we score goals for fame.

They all are very rich,
By earning lots of money,
Some players are moody,
But some can be funny.

There are thousands of good players,
Like Fabregas and Terry,
There are also players of the year,
Like Ronaldo and Messi.

Football is my world!

Ben Wiley (11)
Chalfonts Community College, Chalfont St Peter

The Wolf

We whine and howl and scratch and bark
We hunt our prey in the dark
We dig our dens for when it snows
To keep our babies from the cold
We howl to the sky when the moon is up
And cry and whine when we are stuck
We are the killers of the night
And nothing is worse than our bite
We're sly and strong and keep our pace
In hunting down, the killers race
We are the wolf, the king of all
Even when our numbers fall
And when it's summer, when it's hot
We're threatened to be shot!

Millie Grierson (12)
Chalfonts Community College, Chalfont St Peter

Falling Out With Friends

She was my friend
Now she's not
She calls me names
She takes the mick

Why, why can't she be nice
She thinks she's the best
She takes my friend
She took this girl
But she always comes back to me

I ask her to be my friend
We are friends again
Then an hour later
She's that bully again.

Sophie May North (11)
Chalfonts Community College, Chalfont St Peter

Wintertime

Winter is the time of year,
Where we all bring Christmas cheer,
There's snow all around,
Gently falling on the ground,
There's a snowball,
One, two, three . . .
I just hope they don't hit me!

It is a wonderful delight,
To see all the different Christmas lights,
On Christmas Eve go to bed,
Santa will come as you rest your head,
In the morning, you will find your stocking filled to the brim,
Then you will hear the church bells ring!

Lucy Campling (11)
Chalfonts Community College, Chalfont St Peter

Chocolate

Sweet and delicious,
A lovely brown colour,
Just look at it swirl.

It trickles down your throat,
It melts in your mouth,
Filled with sugar.

It's mouth-watering,
You can have it liquid or solid,
You can drink it.

It is lovely,
So refreshing,
That's chocolate!

Louis Beever (11)
Chalfonts Community College, Chalfont St Peter

Gone

There we were, lying on the grass in the bright, shining sun,
Happy as can be,
I felt different, a feeling I have not felt before,
She said, 'I'll be back in a minute, I'm just going inside'
And then she was gone.
I lay there on the grass, with not a worry in my head,
Suddenly, I heard a car go off fast,
I ran to the gate, but I was too late,
I ran inside, but she was gone,
There she was, timid and afraid, wondering why she left me,
I sat down and started to cry, but there was no reply,
Because . . .
She's gone!

Charley Anne Agnes Kendall (12)
Chalfonts Community College, Chalfont St Peter

The Shock

The shock, it hit me like a boom, *bang!*
It felt like I had nowhere to go,
The tears dripping down my cheek,
I looked over at my dad,
His tears were going down his cheek, like a waterfall
And I ran . . .
I was angry, upset
My dad was moving out the house
Forever!
I never thought it could happen to me,
I had to live a life with me, my mum and my brother,
I was scared, but I knew it would get better,
I knew it!

Gemma May Davis (11)
Chalfonts Community College, Chalfont St Peter

Friends Forever

Friends forever
Me and you
We will stay by each other
I'll never leave you
When we're older, I'm glad to say
I'll still be your friend in every way
I have a shoulder to cry on
A top to lend
A sleepover to have on a wet weekend
I have advice to give
Make-up to do
Just to let you know
I love you.

Emma Shields (11)
Chalfonts Community College, Chalfont St Peter

The Bad Day At School

It wasn't a great day today at school
Not so happy as usual
Got locked in the loo
Forgot my homework
And well, I didn't really know what to do
When I got home, my mum was cooking tea
And my brother was teasing me
I told my mum what happened
And she just laughed at me
No fun to have today
But smiling though
My mum and dad and brothers too
Well, they don't think it's true.

Chelsea Dunstan (11)
Chalfonts Community College, Chalfont St Peter

Dragons

They soar majestically
As fast as they can fly
Up and up and up
Way up in the sky

And look a little pup
Chasing a tiny bug
Fire burning in his heart
Like a little tiny spark

Away you run
'Ho-hay, ho-hum!'
Sings the dragon with glee
I shall have a human for tea!

Tom Barlow (11)
Chalfonts Community College, Chalfont St Peter

Art

No one can explain art
Not even you and me
So when I pick up a paintbrush
I feel glad, but mainly free

There are no rules in art
Apart from don't be silly
You can paint anything
Roses, daisies, lilies

You can paint anything
Chairs, cushions, tables
You can paint anything
A portrait of Aunt Mabel!

Athena-Skye Finney (11)
Chalfonts Community College, Chalfont St Peter

Emotions

Some are happy,
Some are sad,
Some are evil,
Some are bad.

Some are made by angels,
So your happiness always seems to stay,
Some are made by devils,
So your evil stays all day.

All of them are important,
They are like special potions,
The things we need more than all
Are our wonderful emotions.

Ciaran Bohan (11)
Chalfonts Community College, Chalfont St Peter

Love

When you fall in love, you have to be wise,
For all you have to do, is open your eyes.
Your lover might have many lies,
That you do not realise.

Your lover might cheat on you,
But if they do,
Don't cry,
You still have to try.

But if you have good luck,
You might not be stuck,
For your lover might respect you
And you would too.

Yasmin Rahman (11)
Chalfonts Community College, Chalfont St Peter

What A Race!

Whizzing past everyone else,
Seeing them all in my rear view,
They are all trying to catch up,
But they don't have a chance at all.

The only way to win,
Is to concentrate and stay in front,
Because behind, everyone is bumping,
With many of them crashing.

It's the final lap,
I'm very tired from all of this,
But the finish line is in sight
And so is my first trophy.

Reece Tattersall (11)
Chalfonts Community College, Chalfont St Peter

Someone Is Out There

Someone, somewhere, is out there,
The perfect one for me,
Upon a galloping stallion,
Galloping here for me.

Yes, I am waiting,
As you can see,
For the perfect boyfriend,
The perfect one for me.

Somewhere beyond the sunset,
Somewhere beyond the sea,
There is actually a perfect boy,
A perfect boy for me!

J C (11)
Chalfonts Community College, Chalfont St Peter

My Kitten

My kitten is black,
People say he's bad luck,
But I don't care,
I love him so much.

My kitten is fun,
He likes my mum,
He's an angel to me,
But he might run.

He's a playful little kitten,
He got stuck when I was knitting,
I love him so much,
My kitten is so nice.

Agata Zakrzewska (11)
Chalfonts Community College, Chalfont St Peter

The Sizzling, Sparkling Sun

The shimmering sun,
Scorching us to the core,
More and more,
The sizzling, sparkling sun.

The twinkling smile of the sun,
The glorious blaze of the sun,
The gorgeous rays beaming down,
The sizzling, sparkling sun.

The lovely, jolly sun,
Smiling, shining, soothing sun,
Maybe scorching,
The sizzling, sparkling sun.

Trudie Mills (11)
Chalfonts Community College, Chalfont St Peter

First Day

The 3rd of September,
I'll always remember,
My first day of high school,
It was so cool!

It's now October,
I wish it was November!
Then it's my birthday
And I'll say, 'Hooray!'

I'll be turning 12,
But sadly to turn 13,
I fear . . .
I'll have to wait another year!

Sarah Davies (11)
Chalfonts Community College, Chalfont St Peter

Untitled

Violence . . .
Violence is bad as well as sad,
Abusive and cruel can make you rule
Violence can make you cry as well as die
Violence can hurt, it makes you feel like dirt
What's the point of violence?

Friendship . . .
Friendship is good as it should
Friendship's not cruel, not at all
Friendship's the best, it's a nest in your chest
Friendship is a love dart in your heart
That's what friendship is.

Nathan White (11)
Chalfonts Community College, Chalfont St Peter

My Good Friend, Emma-Beth

My good friend, Emma-Beth, whom I've known for years
One day decided to go to a different school to me
I can't believe she's gone, how can I explain how much she means to me?
It's too hard to, you see
The day she left the safety of our well-known school
I could not hold the tears in, but I could not let them out.

Of course, we will never forget each other
And I'll never have a better friend, she has been good to me
On the day we met, we swore never to forget
And never to break up
So, of course, I still remember and we haven't yet broken up
As we still do keep in touch.

Jennifer Cox (11)
Chalfonts Community College, Chalfont St Peter

Little Boy

Little boy stung by a wasp
Screaming, screaming
On and on
No one in this place.

Little boy goes back crying
While his mum and dad just ignore him
Little boy goes to bed
Early in the morning he awakes
Looks at his finger, says, 'Oh, no!'
His finger is bigger than before
What will happen? No one knows
Let's just hope that the sting goes!

Mitko Zyumbyulev (11)
Chalfonts Community College, Chalfont St Peter

I Play Tennis

I n the green court

P laying the exciting game
L aughing and having fun
A nd hitting the ball forward and backward
Y es, you won!

T ennis is a great game
E ven if you don't win
N ever give up
N onsense not to give up
I n the green, green court
S o, go out to play!

Ross Alexander Palmer (12)
Chalfonts Community College, Chalfont St Peter

Friends

Friends are so special
As you can plainly see
They're great for every single one
Even you and me
They will help you when you are alone
They will cheer you up and sort you out, even on the phone
You can tell your friends anything
It depends how close you are
You can share each other's secrets, even from afar
Now you know about friends and how special they can be
They're for everyone and everything, even you and me.

Shawnean Milton (11)
Chalfonts Community College, Chalfont St Peter

Choco Cake

Choco, choco, choco,
Chocolate so tasty,
Choco, choco, choco,
In the blending machine,
Ready to be
Choco, choco, choco,
I can't wait to crush you,
Chocolate squares with sad faces,
Getting closer and closer to being, five minutes later,
Crushed in terror,
Ready to make the glorious choco cake!

Sharnee Budwal (11)
Chalfonts Community College, Chalfont St Peter

Trapped

I am now trapped in a dark and gloomy cave
There are no lights and no way out
I'm scared
I can't see anything
Where am I?
I hear sounds
Scary sounds
Wait, I hear footsteps
Who's there?
What do you want?

Ismail Shariff (11)
Chalfonts Community College, Chalfont St Peter

Sick Day

It makes you feel horrible
And bubbly all inside,
The worst of all,
It makes you fall
Onto your soft, soft bed.

You cannot go to school,
Which is pretty cool,
But yet, you can't move,
Not even dance or groove.

Jacob Barnes (11)
Chalfonts Community College, Chalfont St Peter

Winter

Ice-cold winter,
It's the season of snow,
Full of delights and Christmas lights,
Snowmen standing in every garden,
Smash in the face,
The snowball stings,
The carol people sing.

Shannon Preston (11)
Chalfonts Community College, Chalfont St Peter

I Don't, I Hate

I hate milk
I hate houses
That say, 'To Let'
I hate getting wet.

I don't like people that shout
I don't like walking about
I don't like heights
I don't like having a fright
Don't turn out the light.

Thomas Morrissey (11)
Chalfonts Community College, Chalfont St Peter

In The War!

In the tank every day,
Firing bullets every way.
All the bullets in the air,
But Adolf Hitler doesn't care.
If he wins, he'll be pleased,
Because Churchill will be on his knees,
All the guns killing tons.

In the war, no one was spared
Oh, the war! It's so unfair.

Harry Laflin (11)
Chalfonts Community College, Chalfont St Peter

Hallowe'en

It's glowing
It's dark
It's scary
It's noisy
Kids trick or treating
Fireworks exploding
It's Hallowe'en!

Sinead Hughes (11)
Chalfonts Community College, Chalfont St Peter

Mice

Digging the way out, like a mole,
Slowly creeping out of my hole,

I'm so quiet, you could hear a pin,
But not now with all my adrenaline,

I had seen the beautiful, yellow cheese,
I ran and ran, I couldn't feel my knees,

I opened my mouth and saw the trap,
 I thought . . .

John Dennis Carey (11)
Chalfonts Community College, Chalfont St Peter

Sea

Swish, swoosh, side to side,
Seashells crunch and rocks stay still,
Dolphins, octopus, sharks and fish,
All swim below the massive tide.
Fisherman chuck in their trash
And make this a bad habitat,
For all those who swim in it,
We have to stop it!
But how?

Lydia Willison-Duff (11)
Chalfonts Community College, Chalfont St Peter

Football At School

Football, football is so cool,
But it isn't at school.
People come and people go,
Taking the football, go, go, go!

It's not funny, it's just rude,
People think they are so crude,
They chuck tennis balls and hit my mate's head,
Knocked him out and I thought he was dead!

Matthew Bainbridge (12)
Chalfonts Community College, Chalfont St Peter

I Love My Robots

Robots, robots, all metal and shiny
Some can be big, some can be tiny
Big nuts and bolts and lightning jolts
With a count to five, ha-ha, it's alive!
It has laser eyes and x-ray vision
Mimicking your every decision
Like a secret agent on a mission
It can fly through the air without confusion
This is a robot, that's my conclusion.

Jonathan Jones (11)
Chalfonts Community College, Chalfont St Peter

School

School is so boring,
Homework's no fun,
I hate to work,
I think it is dumb.

We're forced to work hard
And have no fun,
I would way rather be
Lying in the sun!

Isabel Heinel (11)
Chalfonts Community College, Chalfont St Peter

Xbox

The clock ticks the seconds away
It gets closer and closer to the end of the day
I go home and moan because the weather is grey
I wish I could do something, I pray and pray.

Then that green light comes out of the fog
My moans and groans have gone down the plug
I pick up the controller and plug in the mic
And I talk to my friends, all day and night!

Sam Mackerness (11)
Chalfonts Community College, Chalfont St Peter

Choco

Choco, choco, choco is the dream for me
I would eat it every day and night
But I would not share it, not one bite.

Choco, choco, choco is better than my PS3
I would eat, eat, eat all day
I would eat it for dinner, lunch, breakfast and at school
Choco is the best for me
Choco is the bees' knees!

George Boyles (11)
Chalfonts Community College, Chalfont St Peter

Spring

Spring is here
The flowers are out
Green leaves on the tree
Lots of children about
Having fun outside
In the great sunshine
It's always great fun
When it's springtime!

Kayleigh Gingell (11)
Chalfonts Community College, Chalfont St Peter

Swimming

The freezing water has been in the pool for more than a year,
When people jump in the pool, they have a fright,
Some people tiptoe in,
Other crazy people are like crazy frogs,
The way grannies swim, they're like swans,
Some people have so much fun, it's great to see,
Swimming is a great sport,
Do some exercise by doing swimming!

Cassidy Willson (11)
Chalfonts Community College, Chalfont St Peter

Sweets And More Sweets

Sweets are sugary
Sweets are sweet
But sweets are bad for your teeth
Sweets are colourful
Sweets are chewy
Sometimes sweets are hard
Lucky we have a lot of types of sweets
There are shops full of yummy treats!

Emily Picton (11)
Chalfonts Community College, Chalfont St Peter

Sweet Delight

Gumballs and sweets,
Tumbles and heaps,
Of Milky Way treats,
Can't resist,
Just can't miss,
The sensation of flavour,
The harmony of texture,
Just can't deny them.

Rhianna Quirk (11)
Chalfonts Community College, Chalfont St Peter

Rugby

The pitch is a battlefield
Our men dropping like flies
They're on us like lions
Grey and wet, they shoot me down
My best friend comes, but can't do much
The whistle blows, I feel so grey
I've let my team down.

Luke Davison (11)
Chalfonts Community College, Chalfont St Peter

Sweets

S weets are gooey,
W icked and chewy,
E veryone
E ats
T ruffle
S weets.

Kimran Kaur Kaley (11)
Chalfonts Community College, Chalfont St Peter

Tiger

Quietly sneaking through the woods,
Without a sound, it moves,
Sending a shiver down your spine,
A monkey cries, a bird flaps . . .
The tiger strikes!

David Cottrell (11)
Chalfonts Community College, Chalfont St Peter

My Mum

My mum is so cool
Because she's the best in the world
And she twinkles around
Like a star, she's bright
When she argues, she's always right!

Chrystal Faux (11)
Chalfonts Community College, Chalfont St Peter

My Father, The Father Who Died In Battle

My father, a true soldier,
In the war to end all wars,
He fought for his country,
The country he truly loved.

He was a man, a man who truly cared,
A man who both loved and was loved,
A man who risked his life for so many lives,
Leaving behind closed doors.

He was a man, a man who was there,
A man who respected others,
A man who was there to cry on,
He was a man, a man who lived a good life.

He could have stayed,
But would it be right?
He had to go
And fight that fight.

My father was a soldier,
The one that they called Ned,
We never, ever thought that
He might be . . . dead.

Dannii Laine (12)
Highcrest Community School, High Wycombe

Global Warming

Hot, hot, hot,
Cold I am not,
The Earth is getting warmer,
As if in a sauna,
The ice caps still melt,
The heat I have felt,
Hotter, hotter it becomes,
Getting warmer with our sun.

Cooling down I can't,
Going in the sun, I shan't.

Kier Robinson (11)
Highcrest Community School, High Wycombe

The Rainforest

Tall, brown canopies
Standing proud and high,
Lots of monkey families
Swinging in the sky.

Luscious green bushes,
Lots of munchy treats,
I wonder which animal here
Would find it rather sweet?

Panda bear and bamboo shoots
Make an awesome pair,
But just how long will all this be
Before it's barren and bare?

Busy diggers break the mould
Peace and harmony shattered,
Why, oh why, did all this start?
Because it really mattered!

Fallen trees and homes now gone
Where do the animals lay?
I don't expect they think of that
When they take home their pay.

Charlotte Louise Helene Lawrence (12)
Highcrest Community School, High Wycombe

The Army

I'm having to deal with something I've not had to do before
That is watching my cousin Wayne go off to the Afghan war.

You see, he's in the army, in the Household Cavalry
And he's a most wonderful big cousin, who means a lot to me.

In England, he is safe riding horses, horses for the Queen
And London is probably the scariest place he's been.

But soon he will be packing up and heading off with his troop,
So please support our soldiers, they are an amazing group.

Caity Hicks (11)
Highcrest Community School, High Wycombe

Despair

There are places where people suffer,
Places where life is much tougher,
Where children and even grown-ups cry,
Where often many people die.
I never wanted to go to these places,
With no food, just tears and flies around their faces,
Where there is no rain, trees or seeds to grow,
Where rivers and streams will never flow.

How can I make a change
When even another town feels strange?
Is it because I am so young right now
That I can only ask how?
If I was the leader and had my own way,
I would transport water, but not oil,
To these places where people suffer so,
Places where life is much tougher.

Saarah Mohammed (11)
Highcrest Community School, High Wycombe

The Beginning Of Life

When you're born
You have no worries,
Your life is just beginning

For the first few years
You're pampered to every whim
Then suddenly, you grow up
You start walking
You start talking
When you're old enough to go to school
You say, 'No! I don't want to go!'
But you get told you have to
As you get dropped off
Lunch in hand
You see all the children and
Sit and cry.

Xyla Jae Jacobs (11)
Highcrest Community School, High Wycombe

Beggar In The Gutter

Beggar in the gutter,
Lying there in sorrow,
Everyone in the street,
Looking at him in shame.

Beggar in the gutter,
Busking for money,
Everyone passing him,
Ignoring his plea.

Beggar in the gutter,
Cold and shivering,
Growing weaker and weaker
And slowly falling asleep,
Maybe falling asleep,
Forever.

Jeremiah Patel (11)
Highcrest Community School, High Wycombe

Don't Smoke

Just don't smoke,
It will make you ill
And you will choke!

Cigarettes might only be a pound,
But they affect everyone around,
I care about you,
So just don't smoke!

Just don't smoke,
It will make you ill
And make you choke!

You might think it helps,
You might think it's a joke,
But don't forget, it makes you choke!

Henna Aslam (11)
Highcrest Community School, High Wycombe

Death

Death strikes at any time,
Whatever you do, wherever you are,
Crying out and trying to fight,
Will make him want to get you.

Death is beyond life in time,
One minute you're here and the next, you're there,
Death will creep up behind you,
Until he gets what he wants.

Death: it means the end of life,
But your soul will live forever.

Death is always ready,
No matter who you are,
So prepare to defend against his power.

Liam Gates (11)
Highcrest Community School, High Wycombe

Autumn

Crunching leaves under my feet,
Red, brown and yellow:
I kick them up high into the air,
Watching them swirl in the wind,
Like a tornado they whizz,
Round and round and then fall back,
Down to the ground.

I love the autumn crispness
And the changing of the leaves,
I love the season autumn,
It's my favourite by far,
It makes me want to sit,
Beside a roaring fire.

Emily Burton (11)
Highcrest Community School, High Wycombe

The Long, Dark Day

The sound of the guns, the sound of the drums
Draw closer
The snow and rain chill me to the bone
Will this dark day ever end?

I'm alone and cold in my damp hiding place
But at least they haven't found me
I haven't seen the light for days
Do you think they'll find me?

Under the wheelbarrow I am
Feeling weaker and weaker
Thinking if I should give up,
Oh, when will the war finally end?

Charles Basham (12)
Highcrest Community School, High Wycombe

Death

They say death is not the end,
But there is no Heaven or Hell.
It's the nothingness that awaits us all,
Death is coming, death is near.

There's nothing to do,
No food, no water . . . nothing.
Just one continuous drop,
Death is coming, death is near.

It grabs you; it destroys you,
When you want to live the most.
Then that's that, you're dead,
Death is coming, death is here.

Joshua Smith (11)
Highcrest Community School, High Wycombe

War, Blood And Pain . . .

War, blood and pain,
People dying,
People crying,
Will this war ever end?

War, blood and pain,
Guns firing,
Bullets flying,
Will we ever know their names?

War, blood and pain,
Poppies grow,
Before the snow,
Will we ever give in?

Hannah Rendell (11)
Highcrest Community School, High Wycombe

Why Bully?

Helpless child sitting there,
Friends or others - nowhere.
Blood all around,
Pain fills the air.

Confidence shattered,
So are his bones.
Hit for no reason,
Wants to go home.

Tries to walk,
But can barely stand.
Wishing he could,
Hold a safe hand.

Richard Crawley (12)
Highcrest Community School, High Wycombe

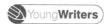

Poor Child

Poor child, lying still by the road,
No shoes, no socks and torn, dirty clothes.
Poor child, lying down in the lane,
Parents who fled - never to be seen again.

Poor child, with tears down his face,
Love and care have no trace.
Poor child, filled with pain,
With bruises harsh, dealt by the cane.

Poor child, now all alone,
Just wishing he had a safe home.

Emma Prince (11)
Highcrest Community School, High Wycombe

Seasons Of The Orchard

In the old orchard, the morning dew is glistening in the sunlight
And the blossom is blooming, the bees are buzzing as they collect the pollen
The colours of the blossom are rosy pink and creamy white
There is a fragrant smell from all the flowers; in the old orchard it is spring.

In the old orchard, the fruits are growing on the trees
As the birds are singing to their hearts' content
As the sun is shining, the leaves provide shade for the lush grass
In the old orchard it is summer.

In the old orchard, the fruits are ripe and ready to be picked
All the ruby apples and the emerald pears and the topaz and amethyst plums
The farmer and his wife have got their wicker baskets and are harvesting the fruits; in the old orchard it is autumn.

In the old orchard, the harvest is done, the ribs of leaves lie in the dust
Jack Frost has cast his spell over the rough bark and wet puddles
The glorious patterns dance in front of your eyes
The wind howls through the air and the crunching leaves beneath your feet give out a crisp noise, because
In the old orchard, it is winter.

Georgia Holloway (11)
Lincroft Middle School, Oakley

Shade

I am the shade, the arch of dark
A powerful oddball in a world of bright.
I am the coward from the fire,
Hiding away at the hint of light.

In the night sky I am constant
Only the stars can shine apart
When it turns dusk, I extinguish the sun
With my powerful shadowy darts.

The elder shades and shadows are
The greatest creatures of them all;
Their iron wills mean they are not
Tethered to a form at all.

When everything is dark and cold
And the sunlight is no longer
Then my fellow shadows and I
Will grow fiercer, ever stronger.

As you mortals seek for me
To stop you sweltering beneath the sun,
Watch out for midnight terrors
They're deadlier than knife or gun.

Take great caution from evening onward
Abroad are minions of the Lord of Gloom;
These shadow creatures are worse than nightmares -
Just one touch could spell your doom.

So, if you wander through the night
And come across us shadow folk
To know if we are friend or foe
The evil are shrouded by shadow smoke.

James Gillum (12)
Lincroft Middle School, Oakley

A Simple Memory

A memory is a simple thought held deep inside a person's heart
It will settle like a secret in a twine of dreams,
But also in a grave of reality,
Memories are what we are,
They hold us up like skin and bones, but can mess with our minds.

One may make the salty tears of disaster run down our rosy cheeks
While the other makes us jump for joy.
A memory can be anything. It could be a crystal in our minds
Ready to shatter and though lost but is still always there
Or it can be the glitter; the sparkle, in a friend's eyes.

A memory can be held but not seen
You can feel it hurt, but it can't be felt
But forever and always it is in your heart
Memories mean more to me than anything else
They can start their own world or ruin ours, but they are still always there.

When I wake up in the morning they're always there
When I break down with tears they're always there
From when I'm playing in the field
To playing in the park they're always there beside me
They wait for many years like a panther ready to pounce or muffle your mind
like a sleeping ginger kitten
They hold me up forever and they're what keep me strong, because
When I wake up in the morning, they're always there.
When I break down with tears they're always there,
From when I'm playing in the field,
To playing in the park, they're always there inside of me
Because they're a link from me to me.

Abigail Mae Saunders (13)
Lincroft Middle School, Oakley

Ticket

My very first ticket,
Ticket number one,
I didn't get to pick it,
But it led to lots of fun,

It helps me keep the memory
Of one special day,
It's just like a diary,
Which I will cherish in every way,

This is the ticket,
That opened my own eyes,
This is not like cricket,
Or tennis in July,
This is for football,
Always the best after all,

When will I ever,
Take the chance again?
Will it be September,
When I get a ticket yet again?
It will repeat everything,
That I have just said,
Who will be playing,
When I will be fed,
For dinner is arriving,
So I will be watching,
Football without a ticket,
But I still hope we win it.

James Guinn (13)
Lincroft Middle School, Oakley

The Hedgehog

I am the hedgehog,
Snuffling around,
Looking for worms
To pull out of the ground,
The moon shines brightly
On the old oak leaves,
Falling on me,
Whenever they please.

I am the hedgehog,
Now the air is crisp,
Thoughts float by
In the morning mist,
Winter is coming,
Winter is nigh,
I wander around,
Under the restless sky.

I've found a home,
Here it will be!
In this cosy hole
At the bottom of a tree,
The sky's turning black,
As the year grows old,
So now I will sleep,
Throughout the cold.

Katy Watson (12)
Lincroft Middle School, Oakley

I Am Death

I am Death
I watch as people draw their last breath
And as their bodies turn to dust
It is in me their spirits must trust
As people come into my cold embrace
I watch as the colour drains from their face
But although in life, Death is the thorn
The souls of the dead can be reborn
The shy turns dark when I am near
And I am what most people fear
Freezing fire is in my eyes
Men assume I speak nothing but lies
Each day the sun sets in the west
And more creatures receive eternal rest
My touch is like the icy wind
And some say I enjoy having sinned
But the truth is, I am alone
When my people went, I wish I too had flown
And all I wish is to be unbound
For in this dark life nothing good I have found
Never been loved, I am just a dark shape
My life is not mine and I can never escape
Because I am Death.

Elizabeth Frost (11)
Lincroft Middle School, Oakley

Dreams

Outside at night, shooting stars zoom
In with the darkness, next to the moon.
Shooting stars light, come down in beams,
Helping with wishes, making more dreams.
But dreams are not broken
If that is what's spoken -
Because in that dark night
All stars shine bright.

Katie Webb (11)
Lincroft Middle School, Oakley

Broken Anchor

Down, down, in the depths of the ocean,
A sunken ship lies in wait.
A broken anchor, a damaged mast,
A story waiting to be told.

Men leap and jump to board the ship,
The mightiest ever made,
Push off from the harbour wall
And out to sea she sails.

Out to sea, far away from help,
A whirlpool beckons them on.
The ship is tugged into the cold eye of the storm,
Dragged down, ever down, to rest on the sand.

The ship is sinking, the anchor's no use,
The whirlpool draws them in.
Screams pierce the night, as fear envelops,
No one can escape his fury.

And there she lies on the seabed,
To feel the wind no more
Dolphins leap and dance,
Around the place where she sleeps, down, down, down
On the seafloor.

Hannah Burnage (12)
Lincroft Middle School, Oakley

Lonely

I am loneliness
Alone in my tiny hole
The darkness hides my sadness
But the light uncovers the soul.

My call is dampened by the rain
But silence is too loud
The emptiness starts to dawn on me
It's *much* worse than the crowd.

The trees keep whispering to me
The pain begins to sear
My thoughts forever repeating
Wishing I wasn't here.

My life has never been like this
It's always extreme
The feeling I most dread
It's here awake, or in a dream.

I feel upset and so ashamed
To feel sorry for myself all day
The wind is howling all around
I hope a miracle will come my way.

Anya Williams (12)
Lincroft Middle School, Oakley

Skeleton

Below the ground I lie to rot,
Till my ribs are brown as the oak bough;
Hidden away for evermore,
Away from changes occurring;
Hidden away from moonlit, dark skies;
Never to see lights sting again.
My gravestone, my protection -
The wet, muddy earth, my roof.
Now I will sleep for an infinity,
For I am an ancient skeleton.

Tom Horn (11)
Lincroft Middle School, Oakley

I Am The Wind

I am the wind;
I watch as the years grow old
When the cold and frost sneak in,
I am the wind.

Only the leaves like me -
But they don't last long.
As I release them, I already know
Their days are numbered.
The hedge and the tree -
For them I'm just too wild.
They think I'm nothing but trouble.
But when the summer comes,
I enjoy all the fun:
I'm frantic, I'm wild
When the summer comes.

I am the wind;
I watch as the year grows old.
When the cold and frost sneak in
I am the wind.

Elise Warburton (11)
Lincroft Middle School, Oakley

What Hope Means . . .

Hope is the bright shining light that keeps darkness at bay;
Hope is the gentle breeze on a hot summer's day;
Hope remains positive when the going gets tough
And offers some comfort when you've had enough.
Hope is the dream of tomorrow,
Hope shimmers beneath sorrow,
Hope is the sparkle from the tears in our eyes.

Hope is a beautiful thing -
And beautiful things will be eternal.
Hope will be there when nearing demise -
For hope lives forever,
Hope never dies.

David Evans (12)
Lincroft Middle School, Oakley

... And That Is Story

The pages fly like birds in the wind,
The ink takes root like trees to soil,
The cover stays loyal even though neglected,
The blurb - an insight into the magic of story.

The author wields power beyond any other,
The power of hope and determination,
The power of hatred and evil,
The power of love and affection,
The power of inspiration and aspiration,
The power of joy and laughter.

By using words the author can create and destroy,
A memory created is never lost,
A dream dreamed is love in itself,
A love loved can never be broken.

As you follow the footprints down its snowy sheets,
Remember and dream and love,

... And that is story.

Charlie Brittain (12)
Lincroft Middle School, Oakley

The End Of Time

It's coming, you can hear it - tick tock
The last tick tock of the life clock.
No water, a drought, no grass, just dust,
All dead, all dark, all rotted, all rust.
The wreckage of the world has been unbound,
Taking life from the sky, taking life from the ground.
As the year so old crumbles before us,
There is nowhere to run, no car, no bus.
As the planet is shredded to ribs and bones,
The last survivors try to hide in their homes.
They hide in their houses, they run round each bend,
But they cannot escape it, the end of the end!

Amy Matthews (11)
Lincroft Middle School, Oakley

My Brother Books And Me

The warmth flows from the crackle of the burning fire;
One side of the girls' faces, a glow of orange.
It's Christmas, my brother, Books and I, read to the children once again,
My pages are allowed to breathe once more.
The three girls sit and listen to my knowledge,
Being read to them by the gruff voice of Uncle Paddy;
Not knowing, or caring, for the future,
His soft wrinkles imprinted on his face; cheeks red beneath glowing eyes.

Christmas comes and goes
Then he is gone.
I am left in his place, a Christmas memory
My brother, Books and I are left to comfort the girls in front of their
Christmas fire.
Within our worn covers, our words warm them
While tears well and fall.
Our words bring knowledge; life's secrets are revealed
Even though Uncle Paddy is gone - his memory lives on through me.

Katy Hobbs (13)
Lincroft Middle School, Oakley

The End Of The End

Flowers start to wither
Colours seem to fade;
The air turns crisp and cold;
Fruits are decayed.

Whispering in your ear,
Nipping at your nose,
Jack Frost sweeps across the land
Freezing up your toes.

Months turn into years
As the hours turned into days;
Time it keeps on ticking
Coming to the end of the maze.

We put it to the back of thought
We think that it will mend;
But when it does come down to it
There's no escape from the end of the end.

Chloe Preston (12)
Lincroft Middle School, Oakley

The Train Of Time

It's blue and wooden,
Rough and ragged.
It's the toy of my childhood,
The train of time.

Down the track of life,
Through the tunnel of toddlers,
Over the hills of school,
And down the crossroads of adulthood.

You can take the normal, simple route,
Or try to do something different,
You can risk it all with gambling,
Or live without surprises.

The train still goes round and round,
It gets broken, more and more,
It crashes again and again,
Until it disappears for good.

Edward Williams (12)
Lincroft Middle School, Oakley

Friendship

Friendship is the invisible link that joins us
Together - or tears us apart.
Hand in hand, we are stronger than an iron wall;
Always there - ready to care!
No hunter can catch it as it hides in the deepest
Of places, that's the beauty of the most powerful
Feeling on the planet.
Drawing out its features helps, but you will never
Touch the roughness and softness of its being.
These drawings won't age but for certain people will.
Friendship will take you on a discovery journey to
A whole new world of happiness, comfort and
Anything else you care to imagine.
Memories trapped on paper - images
Which tell the enduring friendship of the past,
The present and the future.

Harriet Pentland (12)
Lincroft Middle School, Oakley

Untitled

I am the air,
The road on which smells travel,
The invisible breath that drives your life
And the wind without which
There would be no existence.

I am the dark,
The colourless pigment that has no shadow,
The dying devotion to switch on the light,
That nothingness which will grip you in fright,
I am the thing that goes bump in the night.

I am the fire,
The flames that dance against the night sky,
Devouring anything in my path.
The vibrant red and orange waves
Which have such power to destroy.

Matthew Perren (12)
Lincroft Middle School, Oakley

Untitled

Everyone is always smiling
Or laughing so hard
They start to cry
That's my school!

Each person is unique
From the clothes
To the hair
To their personalities

Each person is free
To express themselves
And be who they want
That's my school!

Friends come and go
But one thing will live
The ride we had for our team
Just like my school does

No matter where I go
Or how far I leave town
I'll always be proud to say
St Bernard's is my school.

Holly O'Brien (11)
St Bernard's Catholic School, High Wycombe

My Family

I'm nothing special, I'm just a girl,
I'm not rich or famous, I own no gold or pearls,
I go to a school, not far from my home,
But sometimes I feel so very alone.
I have parents and brothers and teachers and friends,
But sometimes I think I'm the one on whom they all depend.
My family and friends are always there for me,
But sometimes, there are things that only I can see.

But those days are seldom and always shall be,
For I know I will never lose my loving family.

Rebecca Herath (11)
St Bernard's Catholic School, High Wycombe

The Endless Journey Home

The endless journey home,
Felt like it started at Rome.
We began the journey at York,
I just had a big slice of pork.

I was travelling with my family,
My dad was driving steadily,
When we arrived at the motorway,
It looked like a dismal day.

As I saw ahead,
A long line of cars spread,
As long as three football pitches,
My mum gave us all sandwiches.

I studied the environment around me,
Like cars, trees and a Lamborghini,
I felt so frustrated and dull,
I wanted to break someone's skull.

I soon fell asleep
And then woke up as my brother was about to sneeze,
We drove past nearby station,
Finally, the Sat Nav said, 'You have reached your destination.'

Glenston D'Silva (12)
St Bernard's Catholic School, High Wycombe

What Do They Mean?

What do they mean,
When they tell me that I'm useless?
What did they say,
That I didn't belong?
What are they thinking,
Giving me a black eye?
What are they gonna do to me?
Crush me to pieces?
What's next . . . ?
My heart, soul and mind?

Harmony Sharpe (11)
St Bernard's Catholic School, High Wycombe

My Grandad's 70th Birthday Holiday

What a glorious sight
Up in the mountains
Of pretty Austria.

Celebrating
At a luxury hotel,
Overlooking a lake.

With boats going past
A heated pool
Built in the lake.

Cold raindrops;
As cold as ice,
Fall from the sky.

Falling, falling, falling
On your head
And on your arms.

But warm and happy
As your body
Is in the heated pool.

Elizabeth Jones (12)
St Bernard's Catholic School, High Wycombe

My Dog

Gunther, Gunther, you are a dog,
You eat so much, you're like a hog,
Although it comes out the other end,
It drives Kevin and I round the bend!

You sleep with me, you share my bed,
It wakes me up when you jump on my head,
You chase your tail, as if it's a cat,
You eat so much, that's why you're fat!

You attack me and my mother,
But best of all, you're like my brother!

Callum Morris (11)
St Bernard's Catholic School, High Wycombe

Nature

Nature is mighty
Nature is strong
Nature is usually always right
Nature is rarely ever wrong
Nature is beauty
Nature is moody
Nature is smart
Nature always has the greater part
Nature is blue
Nature is green
Nature is every colour possibly seen
Nature is true
Nature is blooming
Nature is dreaming
Nature is in every place
Nature is always with grace
Nature is true
Nature is you
Nature is me
Nature will forever be free.

Luis Miguel Oliveira Rocha (11)
St Bernard's Catholic School, High Wycombe

My Family

My dad, who loves to eat Tic-Tacs,
Shame he can't use the fax!
A hug from my mum,
When I hurt my thumb.
Winding my sister up the wall,
Making her look like a fool.
My grandma in bed with her broken leg,
Whilst my nan cooks her breakfast egg.
My grandad who takes my grandma cake,
With my grandpop who used to fish in a lake.

Charlie Harris (11)
St Bernard's Catholic School, High Wycombe

A Friend

A friend, a friend
I have never known
A friend, a friend
That has shown
A doorway to light
A passage of hope
A piece of forever
And with this I cope
A friend, a friend
I will always hold dear
A friend, a friend
Who holds back my fear
Of all the rage
Of all the hurt
Of all the words
That are so curt
A friend, a friend
A friend indeed
She is my friend
And she will help me in need.

Komal Iqbal (11)
St Bernard's Catholic School, High Wycombe

The Word

You know that word the kids are using,
Using and abusing?

The sound of it makes me jump,
But everybody else's hearts start to pump.

Fists of lightning,
Everybody frightening.

Stop the scratching, stop the biting,
Stop all of the . . .

Freddie Redman (11)
St Bernard's Catholic School, High Wycombe

The Best Thing To Me

The best thing to me
Is my family
They're better than anything bought
Although gifts are great to have
I prefer my family home

Going on trips around the world
From Australia to France and more
My family is a better place
More than anywhere born

Being rich and being famous
Is everybody's dream
But I would rather stay at home
And be as happy as I can be

No matter if my parents are strict
And are sometimes a big pain
They are the best thing too
And that is all I want it to be.

Louise Amos (11)
St Bernard's Catholic School, High Wycombe

Living On The Outside

An outcast I am
They bellow names at me from across the playground
Sticks and rocks pile up beside me
My eyes still as dark as the black sky at night
My cheeks still as red as a rose
I have no love . . .
Everywhere I go, I end up weeping
I run, I hide, I'm too scared to show myself
The words they say pierce through my heart
Breaking it on the way
My mind flooding with dark thoughts
But they stay there as I am outnumbered
Love, I don't know of, but I pray I will meet it some day
That's what you call living on the outside.

John Mark Brenda (11)
St Bernard's Catholic School, High Wycombe

Your Life

After nine (long) months of Mum, you are out
You are free
To see the world
And travel about.
As an infant, only five things matter:
Mum, milk, food, bed and nappies.
When you turn six, you think you are a big kid
And at eight you see life has its challenges.
But wait till you are ten
OMG - double figures = double mind (or so you think)
You wait to turn eleven, 'cause eleven = high school.
So far so good
I would tell you more, but that's as far as I've got.

But whatever you decide
Don't let anything or anyone
Get in your way
It's your life!

Kudzai Gayle Chinjekure (11)
St Bernard's Catholic School, High Wycombe

Zante

Final call for Zante
Greece, here we come,
Dazzling sunshine,
Electric-blue sky,
Golden sandy beaches,
Deserted olive orchards.

Clear, sparkling water,
Bright tropical fish,
Nibbling at your feet.

Steaming waffles,
Freezing ice cream,
Greek salad and feta cheese,
Are all summer memories.

Laura Pennell (12)
St Bernard's Catholic School, High Wycombe

Bullies

All they do is make you sad
All they are is big and bad
Make you feel like you're alone
Isolated in your own little world

Ignoring it is the easy way out
But all you can do is cry
You know you should tell an adult
But you're too scared to tell

You wish they would stop
All they do is continue
Each day it's getting worse
This all started just because you're small

They call you names you don't like
Teasing you
It never ends
Frustrated is what you feel.

Lauren Perry (11)
St Bernard's Catholic School, High Wycombe

The Journey Through Life

Life is so short
The time flies by
Like the evening sky.

Life is so short
From a baby to an adult
From a seed to a plant
You wish it could last forever
But it won't, it just can't . . .
A year seems so long
Like a song which goes on and on . . .

Life is so short, the time flies by
But the worst thing in life
Is to watch someone die.

Laxsan Karunanithy (12)
St Bernard's Catholic School, High Wycombe

The Weird Holiday!

It was meant to be the best day ever,
But it wasn't, because of the weather.
We were going to the Isle of Wight,
But it didn't turn out alright.

As we set off,
Our friend's car went up in smoke.
We pulled over and were going to turn back,
But then everything seemed intact.

Next, we knew we had hit traffic,
Everyone seemed to be in a bit of a panic.
We were worried that we wouldn't get there in time,
But we sat there instead and sang a rhyme.

After that, we had the best time ever,
I hope we have the same journey tomorrow - *never!*
I can't wait to tell everyone,
About the journey we had last week.

Lily Wiggins (12)
St Bernard's Catholic School, High Wycombe

Snow Good

I turned up on the pitch
Fit and ready to go
But unfortunately, it began to snow.

Because of the snow
It was like a white wall
The keepers couldn't see the white ball.

At half-time the score was 12-12
Four hat-tricks on each side
But weirdly, no one had dived.

In the last minute, I scored the winning goal
Against my rival team
And made the score, 12-13!

Alex Gazard (11)
St Bernard's Catholic School, High Wycombe

What's Become Of Our Environment?

Have you ever thought about what
You drop on the Earth's floor?
Outside your house's front door
Litter, garbage and chewing gum
This is all what people have done.

Gases from factories, choking the air
Polluting the blue skies, that can't be fair
One day, the blue will turn to grey
And with that, will come dismay.

What is it with us humans that makes us destroy homes
Only caring to build our own?
Think of the animals and the creatures of the forests,
That like to roam.

None of these things have a say in it
But there is always a chance things can change
And with that chance, there is a flame of hope lit.

Helena Dagnall (11)
St Bernard's Catholic School, High Wycombe

Everybody's Different

Everybody's different,
It's the way we're meant to be,
All that really counts,
Is your personality.
Some of us are different races,
Some of us are different sexes,
Respect is the denominator of all our cases.
There's no point in bullying and physical aggression,
Because then you're just putting people in depression,
Everybody's different,
It's the way we're meant to be,
We're all brothers and sisters,
I hope that you can see.

Daniel Bradley (11)
St Bernard's Catholic School, High Wycombe

Woodrow High House

Woodrow you're full of fun spending every day in the sun
From swinging like a monkey on the low ropes
To all the hilarious, humorous quotes.

I remember so well
Your beguiling scented smell
Of all the pine cone trees
Being buzzed around with ecstatic honeybees.

Blindfold string trail was the hardest activity
But built with noble creativity
Me, being so terrible at my directions
There just had to be a correction
Replacing me as the leader.

The green lady, how can I forget
The lady whose husband was under a threat
Hiding him in a grotto, but not seeing him tomorrow.

Natalie Samasuwo (13)
St Bernard's Catholic School, High Wycombe

Rumours

I told my best friend my secret
But I told her not to tell
I thought she was my best friend
But everyone knows now.
As I enter the canteen
People whisper and stare
I get my food and leave the room
And just sit in the corner, over there.
I wish I never told my secret
As my life just gets worse
Pupils kick and punch me
And some steal my purse.
But as life goes on
My secret spreads
My secret is a rumour now
And you know the rest.

Adel Brooks (11)
St Bernard's Catholic School, High Wycombe

Technicolour Sky

Freezing, laughter all through the night,
Peaceful, just like a dream.
Bang! Fire running through the veins of the sky,
Crackle! Ears popping,
Hearts stopping,
The silent whisper and murmurs of the pleasing crowd,
Screeches of energy, absorbing the darkness,
Dark turned into light by a single flash.
Young children giggle and gasp,
While the adults smile and feel warmth like the burning sun,
All hearts beating to the sound of the sky and then . . .
Boom! The darkness returns
And the little girl is safe in the protective arms of the Father,
It has stopped, it has gone,
That's what they thought,
But it will always be back next year.

Natalie Fawcett (12)
St Bernard's Catholic School, High Wycombe

My Dream Job

My dream job is a zookeeper
Not a floor sweeper
I want to work with a tiger
Instead of a small, slithery cobra.
My dream job is a zookeeper
Not a football keeper
I will feed the tigers every day

My dream job is a zookeeper
Not a ballerina
I will clean their teeth twice a day
And brush their hair every May.
My dream job is a zookeeper
Not a toilet cleaner
I will give each one a name
To me, they're very tame.

Robson Grant (11)
St Bernard's Catholic School, High Wycombe

What If . . .

What if I was not judged by the colour of my skin?
What if there was no more sin?

What if I didn't feel pain?
What if people weren't so vain?

What if there was no war?
What if people cared more?

What if there was no poverty?
What if I could express my poetry?

What if I could show my talent?
What if my voice wasn't silent?

It doesn't have to be enough
But the confidence to say together
We can make a change!

Angel Kula (11)
St Bernard's Catholic School, High Wycombe

The Boy In The Corner Of The Playground

The boy in the corner of the playground
Gets thrown into the bin,
I wonder what he's thinking,
He probably just wants to fit in.

He gets treated differently
From everybody else,
He is forever getting kicked
And left by himself.

He always gets called names,
Like 'baby' and 'nerd',
That lonely, lonely boy,
His only friends are the birds.

Chloe Messenger (11)
St Bernard's Catholic School, High Wycombe

Poem To My Grandad, Up In Heaven

I miss you, Grandad,
Why did you have to go?
You meant the world to me
And I mean that so.

You made me laugh,
You made me cry,
But your love for me,
Touched the sky.

I had sweet memories
Of the past,
Which would hopefully
Always last.

Amy Barnes (11)
St Bernard's Catholic School, High Wycombe

I Didn't Know Where I Was

I didn't know where I was,
I was really confused,
I scratched my nose
And felt a bruise.

Then it came back to me,
It was OK now,
My name was Lee
And I've got hit by a cow.

I got out of bed,
Went down the stairs,
Then something came to my head,
 Oh, who cares!

Jakub Kopciuch
St Bernard's Catholic School, High Wycombe

On My Bike

Pedalling fast
Everything going past
Reach the bottom at last!
Brake hard on my bike
Zigzag snake-like
This I dislike!
Swerve with a twist of my wrist
I can't resist
Being a cyclist!

Elliot Leaman (11)
St Bernard's Catholic School, High Wycombe

Lost

I'm all alone,
I have no one to go to,
I feel like there is no one else in the world,
I cannot tell anyone how I feel,
My parents don't understand me,
I'm too scared to ask,
I get hurt by the words people call me,
Shorty, skinny, I can't take it anymore!

Chloe O'Toole (11)
St Bernard's Catholic School, High Wycombe

My Family

Without my family, I would be nothing,
I do promise I'm not bluffing.
Without my brother, I would have no tips for secondary school,
Personally, I think kids rule.
My family are always there for me when I need advice,
I realise how lucky I am, because that is so nice.
Spending time with my family, brings lots of laughter,
But sometimes it turns out to be a disaster!

Giordano Iaciofano (11)
St Bernard's Catholic School, High Wycombe

I Can Feel The Pain Coming

Why are you standing so near?
Holding your cans of beer.
Why are you holding a dagger in hand?
Don't you remember God's command?
Why are your hands around my throat?
My belongings coming out of my coat.
Why is my heart starting to throb?
You start to laugh with your mob.
Why is there blood on the floor?
My body's starting to feel sore.
Why is there blood coming out of me?
What have I done to hurt thee?
Why has the world gone black?
As I fall to the ground with a whack.
Why can I feel the pain coming?
The sirens whining, the drums drumming.
My body isn't going to mend,
Instead I go to the light at the end.

Joan Laight (12)
St Bernard's Catholic School, High Wycombe

Escape From Hell

Tunnellers dressed like a harlequin
Bright yellow like a tropical fin
Dressed with no convenient clothes or shoes
Hard to get out of here with no clues
Temperatures made the conditions frozen
This place should never have been chosen
Peter found a hole about 2 feet square
About the size you could fit a small chair
A chamber was found at the bottom of the hole
This finding was leading us closer to our goal
Inside the chamber, walls were made of wood
At six feet by four inches the chamber stood
To aid our sight we had a smoking lamp
The conditions inside were very damp
Wood no longer lined the tunnel
Water seeped in as if through a funnel
Puddles of water surrounded us on the floor
The same amount of water found on a shore
The tunnel went down to another six feet
Tension was rising and so was my heartbeat
The upper tunnel was only a dummy
Nervousness was causing butterflies in my tummy
Plunging further down we went
Now I wish I was never sent
Fighting hard to carry on
Thinking of images of when the sun shone
Using a knife to scrape the clay
Praying to God that it would go away
Rising to the surface after 2 hours
The first sight being of flowers
All over my body I felt sticky and wet
My woollen underclothes were wringing with sweat
How oh how, had I gotten out of that cell
At that moment it felt like I had escaped from Hell.

Gabby Marinaro (13)
Sharnbrook Upper School, Sharnbrook

Dear Wife

This may be the last thing that I write for long,
The deep deathly stench that surrounds me feels so wrong,
The sound of maggots wriggling inside of the dead,
Reminds me there's still life ahead.
But dear I cannot explain myself,
This deathly stench takes all my wealth,
And this decay and rot, it kills me,
Though dear I miss you . . . You and me.
But if I was to return to you my love, it wouldn't be justified,
I deserve enough pain to baffle a million lives,
A thousand hearts and a hundred cries,
Because this blood on my hands – it won't wash away,
There is no law, and the disturbed strains,
Cry for me to do my job, to kill a man, but do not sob,
For I am no more than a cold blooded killer,
This war, my love, is no fiction thriller,
It chills even the sickest of minds, to see the bodies, the weapons, the lives,
Just lay there still without a face; this man to you is a disgrace.
Revenge is sweet my dear, good wife, and some day soon I will drop my knife, leave my gun and take off my armour,
Because what happens now is just fair karma.
The sweltering eat eats me alive,
It's become the innocent blood I must thrive,
And I refuse to slaughter some more,
But don't feel sorry because I can hear the roar,
Of the bomb blowing up and coming so fast, I haven't been happier and I wish it could last,
Because now my darling I need not worry, I can hide in my coffin, run, hide or scurry,
And I will be free of the murdering ways, in which focus on us and our Lord they betray.

Lorna Webb (15)
Sharnbrook Upper School, Sharnbrook

Trust

They think they're being friendly,
They think they're being kind,
They don't know what I'm thinking,
They cannot read my mind.

Although they think they're helping,
And doing what is right,
I can't help to start thinking,
This will start another fight.

I fight a constant battle,
But I'm on the losing side,
I'm not giving up this fight again,
I will not lose my pride.

Although my mind is weary,
My thoughts are still my own,
But something is still missing,
There's something left to know.

I need someone to talk to,
Someone who'll understand,
This person will not fight me,
They'll help me all they can.

They will not fight to understand,
What makes my mind go tick,
If I tell them what I'm thinking,
Their judgement won't be quick.

As the battle just gets longer,
My enemy starts to give in,
My thoughts are still my own,
But that doesn't mean I win.

Sophie Hepburn (13)
Sharnbrook Upper School, Sharnbrook

Under The Maple Tree

Why did you hurt me so?
The pain is beneath my skin.
At break you made fun of me,
My scarring is within.
I loved you so much,
What have I done wrong?
Please just tell me I've waited so long.
You tell me we're over, I feel burning inside.
I have to lie down to cry and cry,
Don't you understand what love means to me?
That very first kiss, under the maple tree,
You've found someone else, just tell me who!
I just want to say, I still love you.
I'm shaking and crying,
Like a wimp they say,
Get over him right?
He wasn't worth it anyway,
You're making me angry,
A rage I can't contain,
You hurt me so much,
Over and over again,
Don't you understand what love means to me?
That very first kiss under the maple tree,
You've found someone else,
Just tell me who,
But let me just say,
I still love you.

Katie Holyoak (13)
Sharnbrook Upper School, Sharnbrook

Who Cares!

Just because I'm not from here,
What makes you think I care.
I may be different.
But we are just all the same.
You may be rich, I may be poor.
I may be kinder but I don't care.
You may be faster.
How, how, how does it matter?
You may be gangster, I may be geek.
But for all you know I think you're a freak!
You may be strange, I could be cool.
But it's not up to us.
They are the ones who decide!
No, not us, them, they're the ones who decide!
They could be mean, they could be nice.
It all just depends if you play the games right.
There's only one way to play.
And that's defined by you!
Who cares what they think.
It's all about you.
Not them!
All you have to say is,
Who cares!

Xander De Wit (14)
Sharnbrook Upper School, Sharnbrook

Boy Thief

My bag was stolen yesterday
Stupid thief
I can't believe it
It was just a Niké drawstring bag
What could you possibly need it for?
Stealing makes him pretty poor
He left the books in a neat pile
I like those kind of thieves!

Stuart Reynolds (14)
Sharnbrook Upper School, Sharnbrook

Bedfordshire & Buckinghamshire

Was It Me?

Was it me? Was it me?
Can you blame me for something I didn't do?
Why can no one else see,
How much I miss my little friend?

Everyone looks for me around school,
Knowing that I am involved with the kill.
I feel so useless, like some old tool,
I wish I was invisible.

I see them all turn and whisper to each other,
People calling me names like, 'You old grandmother,'
I try to ignore them but it begins to hurt,
When it's a constant jabbing in your heart.

Some people point and laugh at me,
They say I'm a murderer and deserve to die.
I wish my teacher could only see
All the things they say to me.

Was it me? Was it me?
Can you blame me for something I didn't do?
Why can no one else see,
How much I miss my little friend?

Hannah Bodily (13)
Sharnbrook Upper School, Sharnbrook

You Try

You try and hide from the truth,
But all you hide from is laughter, joy and love.

You try to find the answer to life's unanswerable question,
But all you find is loneliness, sorrow and hate.

Until one day there's too much tragedy,
And life's too much to bear,
So you decide to leave your body hanging in despair.

Eden Smith (13)
Sharnbrook Upper School, Sharnbrook

Our Own Neighbourhood

Why do people do it?
Why do they act like they do?
Why are they so anti-social?
They are the only ones who know.

Why do people do drugs?
Why do they commit crime?
Why are they always acting hard?
We will never know.

Why do people carry knives?
Why do they receive ASBOs?
Why are they underage and pregnant?
Our generations will want to know.

Where do people get their identity?
Is It just from their family?
Or is it from the streets?
Their ancestors would want to know.

These people are from our neighbourhood,
They live around us every day.
Our identities are all different,
So we don't all live in the same way.

Sarah Nash (15)
Sharnbrook Upper School, Sharnbrook

Normal Day

I wake up in the morning ready for another day,
First I have my breakfast, Coco Pops and milk, hooray!
I jump in the shower to blast myself awake,
Maybe a bit too quickly, now I have a headache.

Dressed nice and smart ready to learn, learn, learn,
It is a hot day today I could get sunburn.
Make my lunch for school filled with lots of food,
But there is no chocolate, now I am in a mood.

I head off to school with my mates at my side,
Hope I don't get lost again, I might need a guide.
First lesson is maths, that goes pretty quick,
I will concentrate hard, don't want to be thick.

Break is next; I can see my mates again,
But shortly comes next lesson and it is time to use my brain.
Lunch comes after that, more time with my friends,
Not long now till the school day ends.

Time to go home after a tiring day at school,
Could do with something refreshing and cool.
Relax and watch some TV before homework and tea,
Maybe I'll hit Facebook, but that's it for me.

Jamie Bisset (13)
Sharnbrook Upper School, Sharnbrook

And Then It All Went Black

Friday night, finally!
Time to go out with some mates
Friday night, finally!
Was really worth the wait
Then they turned up . . .

Friday night, finally!
They're coming straight for us now
Friday night, finally!
Running away with the crowd
They're gaining on us . . .

Friday night, finally!
We tried to turn and fight
Friday night, finally!
Did their stuff and ran into the night
Getting serious now . . .

Friday night, finally!
December air's colder now
Friday night, finally!
Wondering just wondering how
And then it all went black . . .

Jamie Gibson (15)
Sharnbrook Upper School, Sharnbrook

Nowadays

It seems we're messed up.
We've been introduced to adolescence,
And now there's violence and drugs.
What happened to the days
When we were young and naïve?
There was never any fighting
And never any grief,
But don't get me wrong,
I know we're not all bad right now.
But to the ones that have changed,
I just wonder how.

Sophie Curran (14)
Sharnbrook Upper School, Sharnbrook

Friends

The ones who are there
The ones who you can count on
The ones who help
The ones who care
They never let you down
We're always having a laugh
Talking about stuff on the phone all night
Always feel accepted
You never feel left out
Always thinking of others
Save you when you're down
They don't make you feel you have to change who you are
They're the ones who are there for you when you're sad
We don't have arguments
They're all in the past
We think about the future
And how it makes us laugh
These are people who I couldn't live without
They make me who I am
And I love them for that.

Ann Freeman (13)
Sharnbrook Upper School, Sharnbrook

Hope Is

Hope is black with a small white dot
Like the end of a tunnels light.
Hope is a hole in a great wire fence
Where you can escape at the dead of night.
Hope is the white dove from Noah's Ark.
Hope is the cool breeze hitting your face,
When you are lost in the park.
Hope is the sound of a rescue plane,
When you are in despair.
Hope is a horrible food when it tastes fair.
Hope is a toy, given to charity
Hope should be learnt in more clarity.

Thomas Tugulu (13)
Sharnbrook Upper School, Sharnbrook

The Inevitability Of Future Ghosts

I overlook a sea front, grinding my teeth
I smile at the distance, cover what's underneath
I bear shackles on my feet, sand between my toes
Shivering at the future, I pray that they don't know
I cannot clap hands, and I cannot close my eyes
I start to write a list, and hope this feeling dies
There are so many places that I know that I must see
Please stop the clock and make time wait for me
I won't be young forever, I watch freckles on my skin
Watch them grow deeper upon youth that has been
I write my name in pebbles, stick them in sand
I'll visit where I left them, memories where I stand
There'll be a house with ivy, and photos on the wall
And us with grey hair, will you recognise it all?
I'll lie out on the beach, touch wrinkles on my hand
I scoped a looming future, but the rest is unplanned
But you and me eighteen, I know I won't forget
Ghosts in our future, but they haven't caught us yet.

Alice Crawford (18)
Sharnbrook Upper School, Sharnbrook

The Boy Next Door

Why, oh, why, am I sat next to him?
He stinks but it could be fate.
I feel that he is infecting me
I'm worried it is too late.
He has spots and nits and hairy bits
And straggly greasy hair.
He stinks out the classroom, he reeks out the toilets.
I would hate to be sat on his chair.
He drools, he dribbles, he snots, he spits.
The worse thing is he thinks he's fit
Oh why, oh why, does he have to sit there?
When he leaves the room there's a puddle on his chair.
Yeah, he's shameful, yeah, he's a sinner
But the shameful thing is I'm looking in the mirror.

Rob Arrenberg (15)
Sharnbrook Upper School, Sharnbrook

A Tree

Standing in the forest ever so free
With all my friends so happy
Then so cheerful when so many people look at me
But then they attack me, so much fear
Falling, falling, crash. I pass out
I'm a rail. I go into a tube, 'Argh!'
Pain as my skin is shed
Falling, I am destroyed into a million chips
Confusion as I am made into a pulp
Then I panic, what is this place?
Washed and then bleached
I'm just being cleaned, this is so confusing
Laid on a wire, smashed into paper
Up and down drying up
Smashed so thin
Delighted that I'm out
But only to get written on
              What a pain!

Dominic Clarke (13)
Sharnbrook Upper School, Sharnbrook

Not Quite Right

A hen pecking at the fertile seed
A hen pecking at the fertile seed
A hen pecking at the fertile seed
A hen pecking at the fertile seed

A hen

Its legs crippled,
Its muscles weak,
It can not moan,
Its life so bleak,

And then a short life over by a bleed,
A neck gashed,
Plucked and hung for a week.

Elliot Jackson-Smith (13)
Sharnbrook Upper School, Sharnbrook

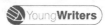

My World

I hope one day, world war will end.
I hope one day, England will win the World Cup.
I hope one day, I will be rich.
I hope one day, crime will leave the Earth.
I hope one day, money will grow on trees.
I hope one day, everyone will speak the truth.
I hope one day, pens will write on their own.
I hope one day, everyone will quit smoking.
I hope one day, every animal is fed and watered.
I hope one day, global warming will stop.
I hope one day, poverty will be beaten.
I hope one day, everyone will be able to understand animals.
I hope one day, there will be no more jealousy.
I hope one day, everyone will be fair.
I hope one day, there will be no racism.

This is my perfect world,
And no one can change it.

Terrell Conlon (13)
Sharnbrook Upper School, Sharnbrook

That's Not Me

Stuck, too much to say-
Can't say it anyway.
Too many problems,
Not enough time.

'Sorry honey, I've got to fly.'

One more minute,
One second more?
Questions, answers.

'No, not now.'

Absurd, foolish,
Immature, naïve.
That's not me,
That's not me.

Amy Honeywell (15)
Sharnbrook Upper School, Sharnbrook

Stereotyping

Give me your money,
I need some 'weed'
Hold my 'just do it' bag
While I smack that dweeb

Give me your black nail varnish
I need a blade
Don't let me kill myself
While I join the black parade

Yo man, give me your love
I need some marijuana
Let's feel the peace in the VW camper van
And feel the good karma

Chavs, Emos and hippies
They're normal at heart
Please do not judge us
Let's make a fresh start.

Jessica Rowley (15) & Clarissa Marston (14)
Sharnbrook Upper School, Sharnbrook

The Life Of A Battery Chicken

I didn't ask for crippled legs and useless limbs,
I didn't ask to be thrown away and not cared for,
I didn't ask to be suffocated with no room to breath,
I didn't ask to be stuck in the dark and not to see light,
I didn't ask to be confined to one space with
Nowhere to go and nowhere to move,
I didn't ask to be brittle and weak with no ounce of strength left to draw,
I didn't ask for hard labour, laying eggs with no rewards,
I didn't ask to be in such bad condition and for my feathers to leave my skin,
I didn't ask for no food, no water, no love.

I am a battery chicken,
I live, sleep and die in this dark and cold room.
I may have many children next to me but I feel more alone than ever.
All I ask for is love.

Ricky D Patel (13)
Sharnbrook Upper School, Sharnbrook

Feeling Strange

I'm feeling rather sad,
'Cause this lesson's rather bad.
And it makes me feel quite queasy,
This way of learning is so cheesy.

Just 'cause I'm unenthusiastic,
Doesn't mean I'm not fantastic.
And I know I'm really tired,
But you know your lessons are admired.

This feeling is quite strange,
How this lesson's so deranged.
This poem, fun to write,
However it may be found quite impolite.

You can make this lesson better,
This time was not wasted forever.
Just put the chairs into a ring,
Let's learn English with a sing!

Becky Bailey (14)
Sharnbrook Upper School, Sharnbrook

Emotions Can't Control Me

I wish I didn't anger and say those unkind words.
I wish I could control my moods so people would like what they have heard.

I wish my feelings would not flood.
Emotions overwhelm me and make me feel so bad.
I wish I could control them and then I would be glad.

I am glad to bring happiness and make others feel good.
I love to be happy and with loved ones I care for.
My feelings may control me but they cannot control me forever.

I realise that I can be
Happy or sad,
Upset or glad.
And I love to be together with the people that I love.

Alice Evans (13)
Sharnbrook Upper School, Sharnbrook

Friends For Life

When I first heard she'd passed away I felt like I would die.
Every time I think of it, it almost makes me cry.
I wish she hadn't left me, I never said goodbye.
But then Mum had another one and my heart filled with joy.
For this one was a better one, this one was a boy.
But after a week of knowing him I liked him no more.
I'd had enough of his whinging so I left and slammed the door.
I ran and ran for what felt like a mile.
Until I bumped into a girl with the most amazing smile,
about my age of 5 or 6
With long blonde hair and dark brown eyes, a funny sort of mix.
I went with her to some swings
We played on them and other things.
She laughed and joked and played fun games
She called me silly names
I felt I had my sister back and all was good again
I didn't miss her anymore, I no longer felt the pain.

Oliver Seabrook (13)
Sharnbrook Upper School, Sharnbrook

When Pigs Can Fly

When pigs can fly I'll wake at dawn
When pigs can fly I'll cut the lawn
When pigs can fly I'll work at school
When pigs can fly I'll stick to rules

When pigs can fly I'll learn to cook
When pigs can fly I'll read a book
When pigs can fly I'll fix the door
When pigs can fly I'll take up law

When pigs can fly I'll learn a skill
When pigs can fly my friends I'll thrill
Until that time I just won't try
Because I know that pigs can't fly.

Tom Freed (13)
Sharnbrook Upper School, Sharnbrook

Feelings

How can we put feeling on paper?
When no one can know what they are,
All this is, is words of ink,
Do the words we write reflect who we are?
What we fantasize about?
How our minds work?

Everything is linked to this 'feeling',
Feelings are impossible to hold in your hands,
They cannot be stored in our brains,
But are they part of our soul?

What would happen when someone shouted out their feelings?
Would they be given the freedom
Or ridiculed for being them?
Does the shape of our world determine how we feel?
Do our thoughts evolve as we do?
Who could be behind how we think?

Amy Bishop (15)
Sharnbrook Upper School, Sharnbrook

Ring! Ring!

Ring! Ring! Went the alarm clock at half six in the morning,
I pulled the covers off my face and got up but couldn't stop yawning
Ring! Ring! As the bus arrived and opened out its doors
I tried to choose the right place to sit, so to not start any wars
Ring! Ring! Went the first school bell that echoed through the school
And my first lesson of the day, was with my best friend, cool
Ring! Ring! Went the bell for lunch, as you can guess I was famished
As I opened the zip of my school bag, it appeared my lunchbox had vanished!
Ring! Ring! Went the last school bell, which finished off the day
I remembered, I only had one piece of homework
and its not in for two weeks, yay!

Ring! Ring! Goes my head at the end of every day
Whilst I'm fast asleep in my bed, my alarm clock gets ready to say . . .
Ring! Ring!

Jazzy Grove (13)
Sharnbrook Upper School, Sharnbrook

You And Me

I am who I am
What's it to you?
You might not like my clothes
You don't have to wear them
You might think I'm loud
You don't have to listen
You might think I'm weird
You can just ignore me.

You don't see me
Talking behind your back
You don't see me
Giving you funny looks
Just because I'm not you
Doesn't mean I don't belong
Just because you're not me
What does that mean?

Becky Heath (14)
Sharnbrook Upper School, Sharnbrook

Sport Is Champion

Football,
2 teams, 1 winner,
Battle for the glory,
Pure adrenaline.

Formula 1,
Tyres screeching, fuel burning,
Who will win?
Pure adrenaline.

Sport,
Track, field, indoor,
Be the best,
Pure adrenaline!

William Slater (13)
Sharnbrook Upper School, Sharnbrook

Racing Day

The sky is blue as the sun shines bright,
The feeling is floating like a kite,
A happy smile, a cheerful race,
I'm running hard but at a pace,
Shouting, cheering it's so loud,
Come on, you can do it, we're so proud,
The finish is near I can see it in sight,
Across the line, I feel so light,
Clapping, hugs from family and friends,
Joy and happiness is immense
Breathing slowly, heart rate dropping,
Streamers, fireworks go on popping,
Achievement is great it feels so good,
I've done it the very best I could,
I run so hard, I run the race,
Now I'm happy and smiling you can see it in my face.

Kirsty Ireson (13)
Sharnbrook Upper School, Sharnbrook

A Cat's Life

My cat sits on a fence up high
Lazily watching the world go by
He watches some people and cars go past
Then he decides he's hungry at last
He spots a bird on a telephone wire
His muscles go tense and his eyes burn like fire
The pigeon swoops down and glides past his face
He leaps off the fence and begins to give chase
As he gets close the bird takes flight
And a massive black dog bounds into sight
It roars out a bark and my cat starts to flee
And as fast as lightning he zooms up a tree
He only comes down when the dog's far away
Then he decides that's enough for today
The events he's seen he shall always keep
So he comes back to the house and drifts off to sleep.

James Holyoake (13)
Sharnbrook Upper School, Sharnbrook

School Day

On my way to school today,
Hip, hip, hip, hip, hooray,
Learning things and having fun,
Six whole hours till the day's done.

Maths is first, numbers aren't my thing,
Using a ruler and some string,
Five more minutes till the end of day,
Or my brain with go round the bend.

English next, my favourite class,
In every test, I always pass,
Writing stories, horror and romance,
Drama maybe, if we get the chance.

Science experiments are so cool,
It's the best thing to do at school,
Heating particles and blowing things up,
Making solutions in a cup.

Music practicals on a keyboard,
Getting ideas from a great record,
Playing in pairs or in a group,
Making sure our song does loop.

Geography last, learning about the world,
Learning how the twister twirled and twirled,
The rivers and their changing course,
Looking from the mouth to source.

Hometime, time to relax
And to find some homework facts,
Home for the night, no more work to do,
Until tomorrow, another day to get through.

Abbie Martin (12)
The Misbourne School, Great Missenden

Three Words

The crisp winter wind
The smell of blood
A memory
    A thought
        A life
Lost in stories forever.

It was a normal life
A normal thought
And now a normal memory
My life was lost on the 27th of August.

A tear
    A love
        A heartbreak
He didn't care for me.

He said it in front of my face
She said it in front of my face
The three most painful words
And with a gun
My pain . . . was over

I love you.

Megan Docchar (12)
The Misbourne School, Great Missenden

You

You were my everything
You were my reason for living
The only thing that could possibly make me drag myself out of bed in the morning
You were the sun, moon and stars, you lit up my life
You were Juliet, Cleopatra, Isolde, Shakespeare's fair boy and dark lady, my Queen of Sheba
Something else breathless
And now you're gone
And I am lost.

Eleanor Coy (12)
The Misbourne School, Great Missenden

Winter

The snowman waved with his woolly gloves
With matching hat and scarf
His carrot nose and button eyes
Making me giggle and laugh.

The footprints in the snow
Leaving dangerous puddles
Some may slip, some may slide
Some need lots and lots of cuddles.

Waking up and seeing the snow
Making me warm inside
Seeing children smile and laugh
A lot better than the seaside.

The school is shut
I'm ever so glad
I'm under the cover
Smiling like mad.

My hot water bottle
Snuggling my toes
It feels so special
I begin to doze.

Katie Morgans (12)
The Misbourne School, Great Missenden

Waiting For You

Waiting for you to enter my world,
Wanting you to turn it upside down.
Waiting to hold you in my arms,
Waiting, waiting for you.

Longing to see your smile
For the very first time,
Reaching for your hand,
Getting so close, but not feeling anything,
I'm waiting for you.

Loving the sound of your voice
But only in my dreams, I hear it,
Where you are is where I need to be,
When will you find me?
Waiting, waiting for you.

I'll know it when I see your face
Touching your skin,
You're what I'm living for
Your steps are the beat of my heart,
It's not fair that you're gone,
I'm waiting for you.

Isabella Handcock (13)
The Misbourne School, Great Missenden

Bliss

Gazing out of my window through my tear-streamed eyes
I think about my life and how I died

Perhaps I lived too long - perhaps he died too soon?
I don't know, do you?

I remember how it happened - I remember too well
In my arms he died and in pain he cried
I felt the heat the instant it licked my skin
And saw him glow redder and become bloodier

I felt him drift away as the smoke engulfed us
I looked up and looked through my window
I thought about how he died and how I . . .
Life is sad, death is bliss.

J L Rutland (13)
The Misbourne School, Great Missenden

The Night-Time

As the moon comes in the night,
Shining into our homes,
Making sure we're content and tight,
Watch the stars and their clones.

When twilight comes in the sky,
The sun will soon arise,
The stars will live and then they'll die,
Then daylight is the prize.

Because the sun does so much work,
It will soon need rest,
So once again for the millionth time,
Night will come at best.

Rebecca Towersey (12)
The Misbourne School, Great Missenden

The Irish Stew

When cooking the occasional Irish stew
Make sure you do it in the EU
The sea's nice and salty there
And there's some spice on the cool fresh air

Don't do it in France 'cause the garlic would smell
Don't cook it in the Alps in case you fell
Don't do it in Spain, the bulls might squash you
And in Denmark the vikings would steal it off you
They won't eat it in Italy, they only eat pasta
And in Germany it would make the footballers go faster

In England swine flu will get you first
And then the recipe will be badly cursed
So the best place to cook an Irish stew
Is in Ireland 'cause they know what to do.

Martha Southby (11)
The Wye Valley School, Bourne End

Colours

Red stands for the blood, running through our veins
Yellow stands for the sun, that sits amongst the clouds
Blue stands for the sky, that hangs above my house
Pink stand for the flowers, that prettily lay in my garden
Purple stands for the plums, that swing gently to and fro on the tree
Orange stands for my goldfish, gracefully swimming in their bowl
Brown stands for the cat, that wanders the neighbourhood
Green stands for the grass, that perches underneath my feet
White stands for the clouds, that fly high in the sky

These are the colours
The things that make us grin
These are the colours
That create our world within.

Bethany Sparkes (11)
The Wye Valley School, Bourne End

Final Goodbye

My cat was my best friend,
I would play with her all day,
She'd sleep with me at night
And comfort me through tears.

With no friends and bullied,
She was the joy in my life,
When my family died,
She became my world.

But then, a week ago,
She joined them up in Heaven
If only I could join her
Life is not the same.

Ceire Warren (11)
The Wye Valley School, Bourne End

Me, Myself And I

Some people think I'm cool,
Some may not.
Only because I follow the rules,
They're hard to follow, my stomach's in a knot.
Playing netball with Cherie and my bezzies,
And reading books all day.
Myself, I just want to burst out.
They don't know who I am,
And I don't care.
That's just life,
It's just not fair.

I am who I am because of everyone.

Isha Turner (11)
The Wye Valley School, Bourne End

Reading A Book

Sitting, hiding away,
Her book to hand.
Nobody sees her,
Nobody cares.
A tear rolls down her rosy cheek,
Then another and so on.
Happy yelps weaken her still,
Till there is nothing left but a large molehill.
Punching hurts,
So too do words.
But being ignored
Has to be worse.

Georgia Scannell (11)
The Wye Valley School, Bourne End

Who Am I?

I am friendly and happy, I wonder what today will bring,
I hear the cars outside my window,
I see the trees moving with the breeze,
I want to be rich and famous one day,
I am friendly and happy.

I pretend life is always fun,
I feel loved by all of my family and friends,
I touch the hearts of every one I care for,
I worry what the future holds,
I cry at cruelty to animals,
I am friendly and happy.

Heather Anderson (11)
The Wye Valley School, Bourne End

Life

When another is born
Another will die
When one is happy
Someone else may cry
Together in one world, made to get along
But some people break the rules, and they are very wrong
We are blessed with a home
And luckier than others
So think about the newborn, providing you with brothers,
If you are not grateful you're going the wrong way,
So be a good person and don't be led astray.

Alistair Beard (12)
The Wye Valley School, Bourne End

Fashion

You either love it or hate it,
You splash out or you store it,
You're a fashion superstar,
Or a clothes hater.
You must get that bag,
Oh those shoes are divine.
I must have that designer coat.
But some don't step one foot in a shop.
Or don't give a damn about the sales.
Fashion is a powerful thing.
It's a bit like Marmite you know!

Amber Healey (12)
The Wye Valley School, Bourne End

I Don't Care

I don't care if you're funny
I don't care if you're tall
I don't care if you're small
I don't care if you're a girl
I don't care if you're a boy
I don't care if you're weird
I don't care if you're a tree hugger
I don't care if you're annoying
I don't care if you're a nerd
I don't care, as long as I've got a friend.

William Wright (11)
The Wye Valley School, Bourne End

My Feelings

I am happy, I am sad
I am angry, I am glad
I feel these feelings every day,
But mostly happy, when I'm away
All day at school, I begin to feel safe,
Because of the atmosphere, and the place.

So my feelings can be very different,
Because I'm me,
And that's who I want to be.

Sameeyah Bint-Mahmood (11)
The Wye Valley School, Bourne End

Moving To Secondary School

Primary goes fast
Then it's time to move
But what you want can never last
I was scared, I was worried
But now that's all in the past
Cos now I'm OK
I work hard every day.

Lottie Kirby (11)
The Wye Valley School, Bourne End

I Want To Go Home

I want to go home,
It's so boring at school.
The lessons are hard,
But I get through.
At break I talk and chat with my friends.
Then next, another lesson,
It never ends.
At 3:25 it's time to go home,
That's the happiest time of the day.

Migle Kuzaite (12)
The Wye Valley School, Bourne End

Sticks And Stones Will Break My Bones But Names Will Never Hurt Me

Here she comes down the hall.
I know I'm in for it.
Her eyes look like red-hot fire.
And I feel like I've already been hit.
I feel tears running down my face.
I wipe them away trying to look brave.
But then she starts running and so do I . . .

Megan Hughes (11)
The Wye Valley School, Bourne End

Who Says

Who says I can't be famous?
Who says I can't be tall?
Who says I can't be intelligent?
Well I can be them all.

Who says I can't be a librarian?
Who says I can't play football?
I don't have to listen to you
No, not at all.

Daniel Cleeve (12)
The Wye Valley School, Bourne End

I'm Different

I'm different because I have brown hair
I'm different because I have blue eyes
I'm different because I am tall
I'm different because I swim for Wycombe
I'm different because I'm unique
I'm different because I'm caring
I'm different because I'm kind to other people
I'm me and no one else in the world can be me.

Charlotte Anderson (11)
The Wye Valley School, Bourne End

Beauty

My dog is called Beauty,
She's such a cutey,
She barks and she barks,
When she goes down the park.

If it is raining,
She starts complaining,
Because she can't go out and play.

Claire Marshall (11)
The Wye Valley School, Bourne End

Untitled

Just because I like cats
Doesn't mean I am not cool.

Just because I walk away
From trouble doesn't mean
I'm not cool.

Just because I don't want
To get in trouble
Doesn't mean I am good!

Just because I like
Skipping doesn't mean I'm fit.

Trudie Reardon (12)
Woodland Middle School, Flitwick

My Favourite Place

You woke up early morning,
A smile across your face,
You're going on a journey,
To your favourite place.

You quickly pack your bag,
And run down to the car,
You get in and belt up,
And now you're going far.

It takes a while,
But now you're- there,
You laugh out loud,
Without a care.

You go sit down,
On that old park bench,
To see nothing but countryside,
Up ahead.

You look all around,
At such a wonderful sight,
Never in a million years,
Would you, here, have a fright.

Your favourite place is here,
Where everyone else can go,
It's peaceful and it's quiet,
Where the river flows.

My favourite colour,
My favourite smell,
My favourite taste,
It's really swell.

This place could be anywhere,
But if you want to find,
You'll have to find a special way,
To get inside my mind.

Bobby Currie (12)
Woodland Middle School, Flitwick

Care

They don't care,
They won't care,
Why would they?

Reeling in the fish,
In their sea-green nets,
Not thinking about others down there.

They don't care,
They won't care,
Why would they?

When the nets are old and used,
They drop them into my home,
Accidental, yeah right!

They don't care,
They won't care,
Why would they?

My children want to play with them,
But I've seen the consequences
Suffocating to death.

They don't care,
They won't care,
What would they?

Have they ever thought of my point of view,
Of what it looks like down here,
From the view of a sea turtle?

Chloe Potts (12)
Woodland Middle School, Flitwick

The Terrors Of War

Blood and bullets everywhere,
Bodies, bones and skulls,
Death is all around,
Guns are strewn along the floor,
And so this is terror of war.

Reef Brady (11)
Woodland Middle School, Flitwick

Fighting

I listen to Mum and Dad fight like mad,
People always wonder why I am so sad.

I sit huddled in a ball on the stair,
As Dad walks past and gives me that 'go away' glare.

As I run upstairs to my room,
I hear my mum threaten, 'I'll hit you with this broom'.

I lie in my bed feeling so mean,
Because right at that moment I hear my mum scream.

As I listen to my dad stamp out of the house,
I roll up with my duvet and hide like a mouse.

As I listen to my mum heavily sob and cry,
I lie in my bed just wanting to die.

When my dad goes off he turns to the booze,
At least then my mum can have a little snooze.

But it all kicks off when he staggers back home,
His cheeks go red like a little garden gnome.

But he's not all that sweet,
When he's sick all over his feet,

And leaves my mum to clean up the mess.

Will this misery ever end?
Because this all seems pretend.

I just want to vanish completely.

Melissa Hunt (12)
Woodland Middle School, Flitwick

Just Because

Just because I'm tall, it does not mean that I think I'm the best.
Just because I've got a big bag it does not mean
I will use it to push you down the stairs.
Just because I play guitar it does not mean I'm a rock star.
Just because I have an Xbox it does not mean I'm a geek.

Drew Gillespie (11)
Woodland Middle School, Flitwick

Cancer

The hospital doors
The worry, the upset
The way it spread
Too big to blast.

Cancer
Too much to understand
The worry the upset
Chemotherapy, hope it works
Your hair, your perfect white hair
It falls like snowflakes.

Cancer
You feel fine
Others don't
The worry, the upset
One is my dad
More upset has been caused
Nan with your cancer gone
You probably know what
It feels like.

Cancer
Grandad get better soon
Sam and I think the world of you
Please pull through
My dear Grandad
Cancer.

Keeleigh Anne Saunders (12)
Woodland Middle School, Flitwick

Just

Just because I don't say much doesn't mean I am shy.
Just because I play my guitar doesn't mean I am the best.
Just because I play in defence doesn't mean I am bad at football.
Just because I like motorbikes doesn't mean I am hairy.
Just because Mr Matias wants chocolate doesn't mean he will get *it!*

Matthew Wright (12)
Woodland Middle School, Flitwick

The Bully

I turned the corner and there he was,
A smile upon his face,
I longed to run, and run, and run
Away from that dreaded place.

But fear rose up inside me,
I couldn't just walk away,
Then he opened his mouth,
I knew what he would say.

Horrid names echoed through my ears,
Then shrieks from all around me,
I was surrounded by bullies, so many of them,
Grinning hatefully with glee.

It was then that I turned and started to run,
My heart beating fiercely and fast,
Then I stopped to catch my breath,
I was safe at last.

But I knew it would continue,
Unless I found a way,
To stop the hurtful bullying,
That cut me down each day.

Imagine if you could help me,
Think from my point of view,
Together we can stop bullying,
Please, I need you.

Sarah Gamble (11)
Woodland Middle School, Flitwick

Everything

Just because you smoke and drink doesn't mean you're everything.
When I said, 'Hi,' you said, 'Bye.'
Just because you have money doesn't mean you're everything.
Just because you punch me hard doesn't mean you're everything.

Chris Peters (13)
Woodland Middle School, Flitwick

Lessons At School

I don't like English
But I love art
I don't like French
Because I'm not smart.

I don't mind geography
It's not the best
I just wish my teacher
Would give his mouth a rest.

Maths is really funny
Because of the people in my class
But I wish time
Would go a bit more fast.

PE is OK
But I always forget my kit
Sometimes I do jobs
But most of the time I sit.

History is quite boring
With all these ancient times
But most of this poem
Is just a load of rubbish rhymes.

I still don't like English
And I still love art
People think I'm good at it
So I don't need to be smart.

Sherie Titmus (12)
Woodland Middle School, Flitwick

Just Because

Just because I am a twin doesn't mean I'm the same.
Just because it's Hallowe'en doesn't mean I'm scared.
Just because I have a detention doesn't mean I am naughty.

Ben Short (11)
Woodland Middle School, Flitwick

I Like, I Don't Like

I don't like school
I don't like RE
I don't like you
I don't like sea
I don't like spiders
I don't like birds
I don't like yellow
I don't like nerds
I don't like fish
I don't like toads
I don't like eggs
I don't like busy roads
I don't like all these things and never will
But . . .
I like flowers
I like rain
I like tigers
I like insane
I like zebras
I like green
I like bubblegum
I like clean
I like autumn
I like fizzy
I like dragonflies
I like Izzy.

Isabel Lawton (13)
Woodland Middle School, Flitwick

Freedom

No one at all
Lets me do a thing
I mean, why can't I?
I just want to be free.

Can I go to my friend's?
I'll only be a minute
I just want to be free.

Can I go to the shops?
Why not?
I just want to be free.

Can I go out to play?
Do I have to stay?
I just want to be free.

I am alone
Left in the dark
Can't go out at all.
I mean, why can't I?
I just want to be free.

They can trust me now.
Now I am free.
Look at me! Look at me!
Now I can fly,
Fly and be me.

Zoe Sparham (12)
Woodland Middle School, Flitwick

Crime!

Youths getting into crime these days
And they're getting the blame always
Some kids drink
They need to think
What will happen to their lives
If they carry around knives
Some people take drugs
Well they are just mugs
Some people are fighting
They find it exciting
Some people smoke
They think it's a joke
Where as some people are bright
They never fight
They don't drink
They're on the brink
Of getting the best out of life
They won't touch a knife
They don't do drugs
Well they're not mugs
They're not a teacher's pet
And they won't want to forget
Their life as a teen
Because they had a dream.

Lee Shaw (13)
Woodland Middle School, Flitwick

Burglar

I think about it every night,
And it gives me quite a fright.
It used to be a happy place,
Before they came into the human race.
People who steal should go to jail,
The police must not fail.
So ring that number,
And make it a happy place again.

Rhea Biswell (11)
Woodland Middle School, Flitwick

I Know

I know I am different
But does that mean you have to leave me out?
I know I am weird
But does that mean you have to leave me out?
I know my friends are a different colour
But does that mean you can be racist?
I know you think you can
But you don't know me
I may not listen to your music
Not support your football team
But?
Does that mean you can bully me?
You scare me
That's why I don't tell
I love school
But you make me not
But soon I will have the courage
Then I will be happy
I'll get my grades
Then it will change
You will have to look up at me
Begging for a job
I know I am different
But soon it will change.

Nathan Day (12)
Woodland Middle School, Flitwick

Are We That Bad

Listen to my words and be careful what you do,
Because you don't want your life to be ruined by you.
Never drink too much alcohol or take any drugs,
Because your life will be shortened and who's there to hug?
Don't do bad things and make people sad,
Because you know you'll regret it, and are you going to feel glad?
So do what I say and you'll turn out fine,
Because if you can't do the time don't do the crime!

Adam Franklin (12)
Woodland Middle School, Flitwick

Don't

Don't treat me like a child,
Please don't let age cloud your mind,
I think, I feel, I see this world,
I'm one of human kind.

Don't tell me I can't do it,
Let me have a try,
Just because you can't doesn't mean I can't,
I do not scream and cry.

Don't let the news tell you
That I am no good,
I can do so many things
That I'm sure you could.

Don't think that you can fix my problems,
They can be quite complicated,
I don't assume that I can tell you
Who is to like and who should be hated.

Don't think that I'm just a child
Of eleven, twelve or thirteen,
I can do anything you do,
My life will glimmer and gleam.

Liza Blackman (12)
Woodland Middle School, Flitwick

Crime

Everyone is smashing windows,
Then running away on their tiptoes.
Crime is always on the radio,
Crime is at it's highest ratio.
Feels like the Earth's at mass destruction,
Why can we not follow a simple instruction?
It is a rule, it is a law,
If you are caught you will be put behind closed doors.
It is not good, it is not cool,
So please stop acting like a fool!

Connor Wemyss (11)
Woodland Middle School, Flitwick

Argument

I know I'm in trouble,
You don't have to tell me,
I can feel it coming on,
You're about to condemn me,
You say you know me,
You drive me around the bend,
I'll say you hate me
Then the argument will end.
I'll say it wasn't me,
I'll say it's not fair,
But please won't you stop
You're starting to scare.
You say do as you're told,
My problems don't matter.
You yell and you shout,
My dreams you do shatter.
I don't want to be bad
Believe me I try.
It doesn't matter if you yell . . .
You'll never see me cry.

Amy Foley (13)
Woodland Middle School, Flitwick

Untitled

Everyday on the radio
Crimes happening everywhere
Murders and kidnapping and people don't care,
Unless it's their loved ones,
Then that is unacceptable and the police must know,
I am lucky it hasn't happened to me,
Or any relative in my family.
The police are getting better.
They solved 10 last summer.
Hopefully all crime will be solved,
And we will be crime free
And be able to live happily.

Tommy Smith (11)
Woodland Middle School, Flitwick

Just Normal People

I see on the streets
I hear in the air.
Do not ask
Please don't dare
The people I see
The people I hear
I follow them to a place
For there is no atmosphere.
They are not bad
They are not good
But to be like this
Then they should.
People, people everywhere
Do not ask
Please don't dare
You shouldn't care.
These are normal people
They are just like you
These are normal people
They are what should be true.

Alex Sanderson (11)
Woodland Middle School, Flitwick

All About Me

I'm always happy but sometimes mad,
There is a feeling deep inside me that makes me sad,
I like playing football and basketball too,
And I like cows that moo.

My dogs are very mad, like me
But they're good at saying 'whoo,'
I like moaning,
It's my hobby
I'm very exciting and great.

I'm always happy but sometimes mad
There is a feeling deep inside me that makes me sad.

Georgia Pain (11)
Woodland Middle School, Flitwick

Life's Not Fair

I learnt the hard way
That life's not fair
It's not fair when
Other people blame you
Or when they are mean.

It's not fair when
People call you names
It's not fair when
They don't include you in games.

At home it's not fair
When voices are raised
It's not fair when
You are never praised.

I learnt the hard way
That life's not fair
But sometimes it can be fair
You just have to know when to stop.

Kathryn Brandon (13)
Woodland Middle School, Flitwick

The Rose

The pathway led to a silver bench
Which lay before a marble arch.
Plants and flowers covered the edge of my garden.
A vegetable patch, filled with colourful foods.
A beehive, filled with sweet honey
An orchard, with crunchy apples
Butterflies and dragonflies
A glittering blue pond
Ducks quacking,
Robins tweeting
The end of my garden
A small area, enclosed
A red plant, sweet scented,
This my rose.

Shannon Ward (12)
Woodland Middle School, Flitwick

Untitled

I've been through the bad times,
The loss of someone dear,
The funeral and flowers,
The water from a tear.

I've been through the bad times,
The illness too,
The hospital visits,
As I sit there with you.

I've been through some times,
The laughter and tears,
I've lost and found,
Over the years.

But as I sit here,
And wish for a while,
I know what's missing
And that's a smile.

Abi Donohue (13)
Woodland Middle School, Flitwick

My Odd Cousin

My cousin is so great,
Because he makes me laugh,
But when I come to see him,
He is always in the bath.
He loves to play his sport,
Especially with me,
But sometimes when he kicks the ball,
He dislocates his knee.
He loves his burgers,
Also with chips,
But when it comes to eating,
He only takes little snips.
There are some odd things about my cousin,
And that is why he's cool,
But the best thing about it, I can beat him at football!

Charlie Cooper (11)
Woodland Middle School, Flitwick

The Zoo

Elephants big,
Elephants grey,
Elephants fat,
Elephants stray.

Snakes slither,
Snakes tall,
Snakes slime,
Snakes small.

Tigers fast,
Tigers smart,
Tigers hunt,
Tigers dart.

Owls large,
Owls fly,
Owls small,
Owls high.

Paige Caroline Deacon (12)
Woodland Middle School, Flitwick

Me And My Grandad

My family is kind and loving
But the best one was my grandad.
The day he passed away was sad
But the memories we share will never die.
I was only 11 when he went to Heaven.
The first memory is when he
Got me my first Barbie doll,
I never put it down.
The second is when he helped me climb the
Step to the small slide in my garden.
The third is when he
Took me to LegoLand.
I was 2 and got stuck in the fountain,
When he told me I wet myself!
The memories will never die.

Mali Ratcliffe (11)
Woodland Middle School, Flitwick

Endangered

Animals slowly slip away,
Unnoticed by the world.
Until a zoologist speaks aloud,
'They're gone!' to our dismay.

But do people realise it's our own fault,
We destroyed their habitat.
With nowhere to live they eventually died,
And they're never coming back.

Now through it has come to light,
We have to do something to help.
Or else they'll all become extinct,
That gave us a fright.

So now we are protecting those,
Who need our help the most.
The animals that walk the land,
As well as in our coast.

Ellie Yip (11)
Woodland Middle School, Flitwick

Crime

The range of crime is such a shame,
Yet some people think it's a funny game,
Although they get caught,
None of them get taught,
That the things you do,
Are up to you,
So don't steal,
Or you will feel,
The hammer of the law,
Come knocking at your door,
So don't waste your life,
By getting into strife,
So lead a life of little pain,
And I will assure you,
You will get a lot more *gain*.

Callum Avern-Love (11)
Woodland Middle School, Flitwick

The Bully

She's always being mean,
And pulling nasty faces,
It's like playing poker,
And she's got all the aces.

She finds the spot of weakness,
And starts to punch for ages,
She does it to others too,
Like being pushed into cages.

It's not my fault really,
Just because I'm smart,
My eyesight is going downhill,
And now I've got glasses, again it will start.

But teacher is sorting it out now,
All this time, it pains,
When she comes back,
Maybe my heart will be free of chains.

Kelly Morgan (12)
Woodland Middle School, Flitwick

Stop Knife Crime

S top knife crime,
T o help other people,
O r at least we will know that all,
P eople are equal,

K ids get hurt because of knives, but we can say
N o, and put a stop to
I t once and
F or all,
E ven though people might,

C arry on, we will still try to stop, so please
R elease that knife from your hand and throw
I t in the bin where you will never see it again,
M aybe you can make someone else throw their knife away, but we need to
E nd knife crime!

Jarrad Miah (11)
Woodland Middle School, Flitwick

Bullies

Mean kids that think they're the best,
What makes them different than all the rest?
Kids that play have to run away,
So she doesn't shout and ruin their day.

Calling others horrid names,
That's another of her nasty games,
Kids that are clever and look really neat,
She doesn't care, she stamps on their feet.

She stomps around,
Like she's been crowned,
No one likes her, she has no friends,
But that doesn't matter, she doesn't care who she offends.

She punches, she kicks but teachers don't see,
The only person that does is mainly me,
She calls me a nerd, a creep, a geek,
But one day she'll be the one that is weak.

Chloe Goddard (11)
Woodland Middle School, Flitwick

Benjamin Laurence Wilson

It's not fair.
He left me to fight for myself,
To cry myself to sleep,
To cry on his birthday.
He brought happiness to my heart.
I don't get it!
Why does it always happen to me?
Benjamin Laurence Wilson,
Why you? Why me?

One thing I know,
That he's safe.
Also in a quiet place.
He's in Heaven.
My beloved brother Benjamin.

Emily Josephine Wilson (12)
Woodland Middle School, Flitwick

My Anger

My anger here beside
At day and at night.
I cannot live without him
I won't leave him out of sight.

In my heart my love is trapped now.
The good memories and the bad
The truth is I need you
Our love makes me mad.

My feelings I cannot tell
So much I love you
I'm afraid what you'll say though
I swear my love is true.

Now you've found your way to me
We can be together.
I'm the luckiest girl on Earth.
Please don't leave me *ever!*

Caroline Bates (12)
Woodland Middle School, Flitwick

Imagination

Black tracks across the page
Bringing daydreams to life
Colour filling in the gaps
Clothing him or her.

Their smile brings them to life
Giving personality
The clothes, they make you wonder
Old or young? Rich or poor?

No dying in imagination
No crime or bad people
Just happiness, no global warming
No rubbish filling roads

Why can't our world be like this?

Kelly Newlands (12)
Woodland Middle School, Flitwick

Will You Be There?

Will you be there when bad things happen?
Will you hold my hand through it all?
Will you be my shoulder to cry on?
Or will our friendship drift away like a rolling ball?

Can you understand what I am feeling?
And catch me when I fall?
Will we stay together,
So I have someone to call?

Will you be my friend?
Will our friendship last?
Can we go on,
And forget what is in the past?

If you look out for me,
Then I'll look out for you,
We can be each other's friend,
We will be a pack of two.

Olivia Parrott (11)
Woodland Middle School, Flitwick

Friends And Bullies

Friends don't hurt, friends don't hate,
Friends are caring, friends are loving.

Bullies don't care, bullies don't love,
Bullies are hurtful, bullies are hateful.

Friends are supportive, friends are truthful,
Friends aren't nasty, friends aren't mean.

Bullies aren't supportive, bullies aren't truthful,
Bullies are nasty, bullies are mean.

Friends are understanding, friends are giving,
Friends don't take, friends don't take you for granted.

Bullies don't understand, bullies don't give,
Bullies always take, bullies always take people for granted.

Coral Harvey (12)
Woodland Middle School, Flitwick

Chavs

They come out in the night
Screaming and shouting everywhere
You can get really scared
Their trousers are low, you see their underwear.

They cause trouble
They should be locked away
They vandalise
They run and get away.

They wear trackies
With their hoods right up
Call the police
Get them done with some luck.

In their group
They're like a pack of wolves
Going around
Smashing in walls.

Adam Tibbett (11)
Woodland Middle School, Flitwick

Teenagers

You hear time and time again,
You see in the streets,
You hear in the air,
Teenagers this, teenagers that,
Blood shed, tears wept
The people I see,
The people I hear,
They go on and on,
About teenagers here and there,
But really, they're not all bad,
Some loving, caring, mature,
Loving family life, with no despair,
So really, they're not all bad
Trust teenagers, they're not that bad.

Louis Brown (11)
Woodland Middle School, Flitwick

Gangsta Boys

They come out in the night
Do not come out, they will give you a fright
Trousers really low
With their underwear on show
Should get arrested by the policemen
Taking the mick out of cornershop men
Listening to Eminem
Are their senses leaving them?
Thinking they're all big men
All their guns going bang! Bang!
Always smoking 'weed'
There is no need
Mainly drugs and violence
Always wish there was silence
Wishing they were all dead
Instead leaving a racket in my head.

Niall Vanner (12)
Woodland Middle School, Flitwick

In The Night

In the night, all was silent,
We're asleep in our bed,
Then suddenly, from down the hall,
There comes a noise instead,
From then on there is no peace,
As we fight to save a life,
For in that room,
A little girl, is lying there in fright,
It's like a living nightmare,
It happens quite a lot,
Every night we wish,
'Oh please just let it stop!'
the only thing that keeps us going,
on those scary nights,
is that every morning, when we wake up,
she will be alright.

Emily Donohue (11)
Woodland Middle School, Flitwick

God's Renegades

A war of attrition,
A war of hate,
To many men,
A dark fate.
Poorly equipped,
Poorly led,
Men are dying,
Not being fed.
With rifles and grenades,
They are God's renegades.
They will crush all,
The mighty and the tall.
With evil factions,
They must take action.
They must call, Satan's will,
Kill, kill, kill!

James Williams-Crowther (11)
Woodland Middle School, Flitwick

Forward

They're at the back of my head,
My thoughts of growing up.
Always trying to push themselves forward,
Like an overflowing cup.
I don't want to let go,
Of the playground of my youth.
But I know things must move forward,
Though there is no proof.
Childhood is king here,
But his reign is nearly done.
For everything must move forward,
Under the eternal sun.
I won't forget my time here,
But now I must move on.
The direction of life is forward,
Till the child in me is gone.

Jonathan Blazeby (11)
Woodland Middle School, Flitwick

You Like Me, You Don't

You like me, you don't.
I ask to go in pairs you won't.
I say, 'Hi,'
You say, 'Bye'
I say, 'Are you ok?'
You say, 'Go away'
What have I done?
You're no fun
Can we be friends?
It depends
Depends on what?
If you go get shot
Ha, ha you're funny
You're just a bully who picks on everyone.
You're not big, you're not clever
You're not gonna get mates ever.

Josh Ramsay (12)
Woodland Middle School, Flitwick

Invisible

Anger, sorrow and pain.
All of them are the same.
Disappointed and confused.
Go on beat me up, but I'll disapprove.
Come on sadness.
Turn from grey.
I'm here with you.
I'm here all the way.
Blue, pink and green.
You're not a queen.
You always blame me.
But no one can see.
The real me is hiding.
But no one can hear.
They just go on assuming.
That I'm not here.

Holly Kirkpatrick (12)
Woodland Middle School, Flitwick

My Unexciting Life

I wish my life was more exciting,
I've read about them in my books,
Vampires and werewolves, witches and even warlocks.
I read about their problems,
Their plans and resolutions,
Their lives and minds,
And in their souls what they find,
Their personalities,
Their lives,
Their happiness they may stab with a knife,
Some, although are happy,
They are happy in their brains,
All their pieces fit together,
None are left astray.

Tilly Currer (11)
Woodland Middle School, Flitwick

Why?

Why don't they listen,
When I'm more tormented and hurt?
Why don't they see,
The pain that they insert?
Why don't they hear,
The spite in their words?
Why don't they smell?
Why don't they feel?
Why don't they care,
That these scars won't heal?
But till I'm old and grey
I'll remember these words,
I love you really.
It's less than you deserve.

Bethany Thompsett (12)
Woodland Middle School, Flitwick

I Don't Want To Grow Up

I don't wanna grow up,
My life is sweet,
Full of ambition,
And people to meet!

I love all my family,
My house and my friend,
It makes me shudder,
To think that it ends!

I don't wanna to grow up,
I don't wanna grow up,
I don't want to be told,
That I'm getting older,
And older means old!

Lauren Wiles (11)
Woodland Middle School, Flitwick

Tell A Teacher!

They strut around thinking they're the best,
When really they're a bug squashed on a car.
They will threaten you,
It sometimes drives you to the brink of death!

They will bully any kind of group,
From nerds to emos, chavs to plastics.
But all these have something in common,
They've all been bullied!

Let me give you a tiny bit of advice,
I bet you have been bullied,
You just don't know it.
Always remember,
Tell a teacher!

Saskia Underwood (12)
Woodland Middle School, Flitwick

Crime

I think about it day and night
I know that something's not quite right
The world used to be such a happy place
Then we came, the human race
There're criminals everywhere you look
Even in your favourite book.

When you go into town
You have to watch your money
Even when it's nice and sunny
But if we work together we can make the world a better place to be
Get to know people, invite them round for tea
So next time you see crime
Ring nine, nine, nine.

Aimée Bishop (11)
Woodland Middle School, Flitwick

Why?

I hear names being called from the dusty street.
I see drugs to the side of the cold alley.
I smell alcohol, wafting through the damp night air
But why, why does this happen?
I hear racist remarks,
I see graffiti, of evil words on the walls,
But why, why does this happen?
I hear bullying – words I have never dreamed of using.
I see litter, polluting the worlds around me,
So why, why does this happen?
I hear piercing screams,
I see people with knives,
So why does this happen? Why, why, why?

Katie Daw (12)
Woodland Middle School, Flitwick

Why?

Bullying to children and adults is not cool,
In fact it is very cruel,
Children in the playground not having friends
Boys and girls not keeping up with new fashion trends.
Why do it? People ask, what have I done to you?
Name-calling and punches in the playground,
Children falling on the floor trying not to make a sound.
All this leads to making a child depressed and mentally down.
We have to stop this before it's too late.
We have to stop this pure hate.
Tell a teacher, tell a friend.
So that their heart can mend.
'Why do it?' I said, 'I have done nothing to you.'

Laura Burgess (12)
Woodland Middle School, Flitwick

Dreams

In my dreams, I see horrible things.
In my dreams, I see relatives die.
In my dreams, I get scared.
In my dreams, I see a masked killer.
In my dreams, I hear screaming.
In my dreams, the killer reveals himself.
In my dreams, the killer is me.
In my dreams, I am the key.
In my dreams, I see no light.
In my dreams, I feel no empathy.
In my dreams, I feel no mercy.
In my dreams, I see no trees.
In my dreams, I am the nightmare of my dreams.

Daniel Keegan (12)
Woodland Middle School, Flitwick

Someone

Is there someone sad and lonely?
Is there someone hurt and broken hearted?
Is there someone flooding with fears?
Is there someone getting abused?
Is there someone who got hurt through friendship?
Is there someone stressed and annoyed?
Is there someone in a fight?
Is there someone getting bullied?

Is there a way of stopping this happening?
Is there a way to stop these negative things?

There is a way to stop this happening!
There is a way to stop these negative things!

Amber Walker (12)
Woodland Middle School, Flitwick

Glad!

You think we are bad,
You think we are sad,
You say we may take drugs,
You say we may be thugs.

You say we could be killers,
But that does not thrill us,
You think that we smoke,
That is true to you old folk.

At the end of the day,
We are not bad,
We are happy,
We are glad!

Ryan Pickard (11)
Woodland Middle School, Flitwick

I Hear, I See, I Smell

I hear the names being called,
In the freezing cold,
I see these people taking drugs, being thugs,
I smell the smoke, as people choke,
But why are you wrecking your lives is what I want to know?

I hear people swearing,
That's daring!
I see people drinking,
They're not thinking,
I smell the fear as I pass a group,
I want to go around them in a loop
Why are you wrecking your lives is what I want to know?

Kayleigh Lyon (11)
Woodland Middle School, Flitwick

My Mate

Shopping is great,
Especially with my mate
She makes me laugh
While we run around being daft
In and out of shops we go
The time goes fast but kind of slow.

Playing with my mate
Is especially great
I love it when she comes round
When Dad complains about the sound,
That's all that matters,
Because my mate is great.

Lauren Ash (11)
Woodland Middle School, Flitwick

Uniform

We may seem all the same, but we all have different lives
The lives of children changed, conformity causing them strife.

No one could survive a journey to our souls
But to adults our souls are all the same, no changes at all.

To them we are strangers, no uniforms and no change
A bunch of mindless zombies and mindless all the same.

They are strangers to the children and rulers over all.
To them we are white or black, matching bricks in the wall.

We are covered in oppression, being hammered down,
Soldiers in matching uniform, suffering without a sound.

Jamie Dann (11)
Woodland Middle School, Flitwick

Hate

'Hate' is a strong word.
It cannot always be heard.
Some people say it rocks,
But it gives me the shocks.

Hate is definitely not my mate.
I always ignore it when I go to the fête
I jig and I jag
But I lost my bag,
'Oh I hate that bag,' I say
I realise that hate,
Is now my very best mate!

Stephanie Fox (12)
Woodland Middle School, Flitwick

My Life Is . . .

My life is full of freedom
My life is full of hope
My life is full of lots of things
Just because I can cope.

Others' lives are worse than mine
I give the things they might need
It's just that most of the time
I think I do the right deed.

In life I want to go far
I want to reach for the stars.

Heléna Batchelor (11)
Woodland Middle School, Flitwick

My Sisters And Me

Anna is never glum,
She likes a lot of fun,
Anna loves her mum.

Catherine likes to dance a lot,
She also sings and sings.
She joins in my adventure games of
Castles, knights and kings.

My sisters sometimes drive me mad,
They never make me sad.
But I am very glad to be their big brother.

Thomas Andrew Lark (11)
Woodland Middle School, Flitwick

Just Because

Just because some people hurt you, doesn't mean everyone does.
Just because I'm shy, doesn't mean I can't be loud.
Just because I don't smoke, doesn't mean I'm not cool.
Just because I read thick books, doesn't make me a nerd.
Just because I don't really like animals, doesn't mean I want to hurt them.
Just because I don't like parties, doesn't mean I don't like music
and dancing.
Just because I don't like fighting, doesn't mean I'm not strong.
I do what I want to do.
And no one can change that.

Holly Plenty (12)
Woodland Middle School, Flitwick

Autumn

Silence at night,
Darkness all around,
A beam of light.
The sound of the waves swishing here and there,
The leaves floating along in a pair,
Falling off the tree from the windy air.
The multi-colours of autumn have arrived,
The piles of leaves into which we dive.
Autumn is a time to rejoice,
The start of winter is not a choice.

Aimee Hutchinson (11)
Woodland Middle School, Flitwick

Bedfordshire & Buckinghamshire

She Is MY Friend

I love her so much.
She helps me with my work.
She is there when I am sad.
She is always there for me.
I am going to miss her!
I am going to miss her, when she smiles.
I would like to see her all the time.
She is the best!
I will never forget her, never.
She is my friend!

Charlotte Lucy Wermerling (12)
Woodland Middle School, Flitwick

Lemons Or Choc?

Sweet or sour?
Nice or not?
Would you like lemon or choc?

Rich or a high-pitch?
Sour or feeling like power?
Would you like lemons or choc?

Feeling happy or being yappy?
Feeling high or being low?
Would you like lemons or choc?

Thomas Woodcraft (11)
Woodland Middle School, Flitwick

Bullying Wounds The Soul

Suddenly it just happened
I don't know why it did,
They push me,
They shove me,
They push me in the ditch.

They say words will never hurt you,
I think this statement is not true,
They stay with you forever,
So why are they so cruel?

Anna Bright (12)
Woodland Middle School, Flitwick

Am I The Only One?

Am I the only one that feels invisible?
Am I the only one that is vulnerable?
Am I the only one who can see what is going on?
Am I the only one that cares?

Do I really have to have certain things to be cool?
Or am I just unacceptable?

Do you feel the same
Or am I the only one?

Isaac Malkani (11)
Woodland Middle School, Flitwick

My Life

Just because I live at the back
Of Flitwick doesn't mean I'm a bad person.
Just because I like PE
Doesn't mean I like all sports.
Just because I like sweets and chocolate
Doesn't mean I am fat.
Just because I like animals
Doesn't mean I eat them very often.

Zoe Burton (11)
Woodland Middle School, Flitwick

Just Because I

Just because I don't play out, doesn't mean nobody likes me.
Just because I do the work, doesn't mean I am a geek.
Just because people make me angry, doesn't mean I'm never calm.
Just because I hide away, doesn't mean I'm a wimp.
Just because people hate me, doesn't mean I don't like anyone.
Just because people disappoint me, doesn't mean I'm never excited.
You can think what you want
But this is just me.

Megan Darvall (12)
Woodland Middle School, Flitwick

Maybe

Maybe I don't want to get drunk 24/7
Maybe I just want to go to Heaven.
Maybe I don't want to live off benefits
Maybe I just want to get on with it!
Maybe you don't want to be quiet
Maybe if you do you could be a pilot
Maybe if you don't do these bad things
Your light bulb 'may ting.'

Mitchell Flewers (12)
Woodland Middle School, Flitwick

My Jiggalow

My life is nothing without him,
Only death could break our bond,
I still see his eyes, the way he looked at me,
I see us galloping through meadows, we were a team you see.
My pony was amazing, but deep down I know he still cares about me.
Our bond is now broken, we were separated, I hate every moment of us being apart, it is horrid.
I dream of riding him again, of seeing him again . . .

Lucy Elizabeth Rollinson (11)
Woodland Middle School, Flitwick

My Life

My life is a fairy tale.
But I hate to admit it.
My life is a bunch of flowers.
But I hate to be stung.
My life is a colourful wave.
But black is OK.
Outside I am grumpy,
But really I am kind.

Charlotte Wood (11)
Woodland Middle School, Flitwick

Football Problems

All the money
All the time
And the credit crunch.

All the money goes to waste
By kicking a ball
By wearing boots
By scoring a goal.

Tyler Callum Webb (11)
Woodland Middle School, Flitwick

Bust-A-Rhyme - Bedfordshire & Buckinghamshire

Young Writers Information

We hope you have enjoyed reading this book - and that you will continue to enjoy it in the coming years.

If you like reading and writing poetry drop us a line, or give us a call, and we'll send you a free information pack.

Alternatively if you would like to order further copies of this book or any of our other titles, then please give us a call or log onto our website at www.youngwriters.co.uk

Young Writers Information
Remus House
Coltsfoot Drive
Peterborough
PE2 9JX
(01733) 890066